THE HISTORY
EMOTIONS

THE HISTORY OF EMOTIONS

A Student Guide to Methods and Sources

Katie Barclay

First published 2020 by
RED GLOBE PRESS

Red Globe Press in the UK is an imprint of Macmillan Education Limited, registered in England, company number 01755588, of 4 Crinan Street, London, N1 9XW.

Red Globe Press® is a registered trademark in the United States, the United Kingdom, Europe and other countries.

ISBN 978-1-352-01037-4 hardback

ISBN 978-1-352-01035-0 paperback

This book is printed on paper suitable for recycling and made from fully managed and sustained forest sources. Logging, pulping and manufacturing processes are expected to conform to the environmental regulations of the country of origin.

A catalogue record for this book is available from the British Library.

A catalog record for this book is available from the Library of Congress.

Contents

Acknowledgements

This book was developed during my time at the University of Adelaide, working with the Department of History and ARC Centre of Excellence in the History of Emotions. It was inspired by my undergraduate students in my Emotions in Historical Perspective course; I'd like to thank them for letting me try out the material on them and giving me useful feedback on how to develop it. Both my teaching and scholarship in the History of Emotions have been wonderfully supported by my colleagues both at Adelaide and in the Centre, and I thank them for their contributions to my thinking on this topic. I particularly thank Amy Milka, Mark Neuendorf, Jade Riddle and Abaigeal Warfield for their guest lectures in my courses, enriching the topic for me and the students, and to Meagan Nattrass for her comments on Chap. 6. Amy Milka gets particular mention too for her research assistance on this project, for her comments on various chapters, and for being a gracious colleague and lunch-buddy.

List of Illustrations

1 The History of Emotions: An Introduction

To feel is a critical capacity of the human and perhaps other species too. Our emotions, as we call them at this historical moment, are not just an unthinking biological response to our environment, but part of how we engage with and interpret the world. To feel, even strongly or passionately, forms an important part of our judgement; our feelings direct us to whether something is right, wrong, safe or dangerous. Because of this, they are fundamentally social actions – how we respond to something in our environment is a learned behaviour. Our reaction to seeing a tiger depends on not only whether it is in a zoo or running loose in the middle of New York but also whether we have been given the skills and capacities to manage an encounter with a tiger. A zookeeper or hunter might encounter a tiger with different feelings than a person walking out of a shop, carrying their latest purchase. How we explain our emotional response to the tiger is also shaped by language. Different languages, and languages at different historical periods, incorporate a range of emotion words that provide a vocabulary for feeling, but not only do words vary across languages and time, but what they mean changes too. A person who expresses fear at meeting a tiger might not mean, or even feel, the same thing as a person from a very different time period or place. The history of emotions is a body of scholarship that explores this variation in the experience, understanding and expression of emotion in different times and places. It seeks to ask what difference such variety in emotional experience means not just for the individual who feels, but for the societies in which they live.

Uncovering emotions and how they shape the past requires a set of tools or methodologies, a skillset that the historian brings to their historical sources to aid with analysis. This book introduces some of the principal tools used by historians of emotion today and offers some practical guidance on how they can be applied to historical sources. Chapters 2, 3, 4, 5, 6 and 7 each explore a particular concept or method in the field, before offering a case study of how such a concept can be deployed to further understanding of emotions in historical context. To help readers apply these methods themselves, case studies consist of some helpful background context, some primary sources for analysis, and some guiding questions to get people started. When working on your own project, wider reading of the academic scholarship on the topic would typically provide the background context for a study of a set of sources. Chapter conclusions offer some brief findings of the sorts of information we might draw from a particular case study to help readers assess their own findings; readers may find they draw different conclusions. That's how historical debates begin! For readers who wish to go further in the field, Chap. 8 surveys some key areas of current research. Across the volume, chapters also provide additional reading to allow further knowledge and understanding of the topic. Key readings on the topic are starred in further reading lists.

This chapter asks what we mean by emotion, before introducing the history of emotion and then explores what we mean by a concept, methodology or theory within the discipline of history and why historians think that they are important. Many of the general principles introduced here apply to any field of history, offering a useful skillset for general historical research. But the history of emotions also raises some particular problems of its own, and this book equips students to manage them.

WHAT IS AN EMOTION?

The nature of an emotion, or emotion in general, is a topic of considerable controversy that ranges across the biological sciences, psychology and the humanities. It has been an ongoing debate now for at least a millennium as each era and society brought their own thinkers to the question. This book does not, indeed cannot, answer this question. Instead it offers some key terms and concepts used by people exploring this question. 'Emotion' is a relatively new word. Whilst its origins can be traced back to medieval French, for much of the early modern period it was a term that suggested movement or motion, particularly of groups or crowds. It was not until the nineteenth century that it came to be regularly deployed in the way that it is today – to refer to an amorphous category of 'felt' experiences.[1]

Historians of emotions sometimes use emotion in this general sense, but more often they use it as a technical term to refer to felt experiences that have been named or labelled, like 'love' or 'anger'. This distinguishes emotion from 'affect' and 'feeling'. Feeling is a word used to describe the personal experience of emotion in the body. Importantly, feelings – a bit like emotions – are something that the individual has acknowledged and identified, even if they have not yet given them a specific name (we might feel 'emotional'). Affect however, is 'prediscursive'; it is the experience of emotion before it is claimed and named. It is often thought of in terms of 'intensities', a heightening of senses or sensitivity to environment, felt as a shift in emotional state away from calmness. For some biological scientists, this idea is important as they see affect as a biological tool that helps living things operate in the world; an animal might sense danger, for example, and can respond even though they do not have language and cannot name such danger.[2] For other scholars, affect can be an important idea to explain a broad range of embodied experiences that go unnamed or unacknowledged, perhaps experienced unconsciously. An example might be walking into a room of very anxious people, and without realising it becoming anxious too, so that when a colleague walks in you respond grumpily to them. This grumpiness can be explained – by your anxiety – but the change in your emotional state happened without you being consciously aware of it.

EMOTIONS AND LANGUAGE

These definitions of emotion, feeling and affect are a specialist language of the field, and do not always correspond to everyday uses of the terms or indeed usages in other fields, especially the sciences. They reflect some key debates within the humanities about the nature of human experience, and particularly the importance of language in shaping experience. Especially since the post-structuralist turn of the 1980s and 1990s, language – the words we deploy and the rules that shape how they are used – has been understood as critical to how human beings interpret their experience. Words are not neutral descriptors of the things they describe, but order the world, placing things in particular categories, adding 'valence' (that is, whether it is viewed as a good or bad thing) and producing systems of logic and 'common sense'.

The word 'tiger' is used to describe – at least most of the time – a large orange and black stripy cat. There is no innate reason why a tiger should be called a tiger; this was a label given to it by humans. However once named, the word 'tiger' brings with it a set of associated meanings that shape how we understand what the tiger is. The word 'tiger' conveys a particular image to the reader, a pictorial representation, and it draws on an associated set of characteristics. One reader on hearing the word 'tiger' might envision Tigger from *Winnie-the-Pooh*; another might remember a live tiger viewed when visiting India. The characteristics of the tiger might be physical – orange, black, stripes, four legs, fluffy – but also more abstract. Tigers might bring to mind power, grace, speed, fear or awe. They might also evoke pity or sadness, if placed in the context of their increasing rarity and vulnerability.

How the reader interprets the word 'tiger' then depends on the context in which the word appears – an account of a gracious hunter leaping on its prey in a jungle or muzzled with mangy fur in a zoo – and also their experience with tigers. An illiterate medieval Englishwoman may have never encountered the term 'tiger' and so would hear only an unfamiliar word. An early modern Indian might associate tigers with leadership and 'kingly' qualities, and a Buddhist might recognise the tiger as a symbol of anger. A villager whose flocks were harassed by tigers might view them negatively, seeing them as a danger or nuisance. A conservationist might only see a beautiful, noble creature. The impact of these complex associations with both the term tiger and the animal itself mean that an early modern Indian who encountered a tiger in a street might respond differently to a modern New York shopper. Words, and their placement in a system of associated meanings, shape our engagement with the world around us.

This emphasis on language as representational – that is, not an innate quality of the thing described – led many theorists to separate language from the material, the physical structures that exist around us and which we label with words. This division between words and things has been a critical site of debate and discussion within a wide range of humanities fields over the last century. What is the relationship between the two and how do we manage the gap between? At an extreme end, some argue that there is nothing beyond the representational, that – at least for humans – words produce the world. Others seek to give varying amounts of agency to the material world. This might be to say that at least part of how we interpret 'the tiger' is shaped by the creature which we have named tiger, that their shape, behaviour, relationship to humans contribute to our understanding of 'tiger'. How much agency should be given to 'the material' is a topic of significant debate.[3] Others again seek to recognise that there are material experiences that effectively operate beyond language, that exist independently of the human – we are not the centre of the universe.

EMOTIONS, COGNITION AND THE BODY

Affect is an experience that is often thought to pre-exist language. Many affect theorists, building on this distinction between the word and the thing, place the material body and our emotional responses to our environments on the 'thing' side. Some, but certainly not all, tie this into hard-wired biological responses that are remnants of our evolutionary history. This is associated with a group of scientists who posit the concept of 'basic emotions'. Basic emotions theory suggests that, while many emotions are products of human culture and learned behaviour, others are hard-wired and found in every culture. There is some debate over what should be on the list of 'basic' emotions, but fear, disgust, anger and happiness are popular. Not all affect theorists subscribe to these ideas; some are more interested in labelling bodily experiences that humans struggle to recognise or name and especially to address behaviours that appear to be relatively 'unthinking', such as the heightened energy produced by the crowd at a rock festival.

Some historians of emotion dislike the concept of 'affect' and not just because they are suspicious of the idea that there are things that exist beyond language. Some are concerned that the emotion–affect distinction parallels an emotion–cognition division, where our emotional experiences are distinguished from thought or reason. That emotion and reason are distinct faculties has been critical to the conceptualisation of emotion in the West since the early modern period. One of the results of this has been that reason is often placed as the human faculty that moderates or manages emotional experience. Emotions are sometimes envisioned along a 'hydraulic' model, things waiting to burst out from the human and requiring continual management. Yet, this idea is far from universal – even as it was posited by some medical thinkers in western Europe, others were contesting this model, emphasising the role of imagination (the mind or thought) in producing emotional experiences. Current thinking on this topic emphasises that emotion and cognition operate in parallel with each other, reciprocally shaping human bodily experience. This means that, when our body encounters a tiger, both our education and training and our emotions operate together to produce our response. If I am a hunter, I do not first feel fear and then apply reason to control my emotion; rather my immediate emotional response reflects that I am an experienced hunter. If this is the case, then affect becomes a problematic idea, as no bodily experience exists independently of thought, of the layers of 'culture' that shape how we respond to the world. Despite this, many people find it a helpful term for engaging with bodily experiences that are challenging to name or describe, or which are more abstract or amorphous.

EMOTIONS AND THE GROUP

One of the impacts of a focus on language and thought in the production of emotion is that emotion is no longer just something associated with individuals and the personal. Even if our own idiosyncratic experiences and upbringing make us unique from the next person, the language that we share with others in our community – the communal agreement that tigers are tigers and that we should run away (or not) when we see tigers – influences how we experience the world emotionally. That language is produced by groups – and not individuals – ensures emotion, given form by language, becomes a social and shared activity. This is not to say that everyone in the same culture responds identically to the same situation. Just as hunters and shoppers might have different reactions to meeting a tiger because of their training and experience, so too do individuals bring a range of cultural training and capacities to their emotional experiences.

Some of these things can be quite personal to individuals or small groups (like learning to hunt), but some can be critical social divisions. Many cultures associate different emotional qualities with men and women, for example, typically expecting women to be more emotional, less able to control their embodied experiences. Children and youth across many cultures are expected to be more emotional than adults, whilst justifications for social hierarchies based on race, class and caste have often deployed ideas about emotion to enforce such beliefs. Nor has being emotional always been seen as problematic in these productions of hierarchy. Since the eighteenth century, emotional range, sophistication and public expression have been associated with the elite in Europe, while the working class have been portrayed as 'hard' and so less civilised. These are stereotypes, of course, not people's personal experience of emotion. Yet, stereotypes are not entirely removed from human experience. That women were allowed to be more emotional in public often gave them more permission to do so and not be stigmatised.

Women were able to use these opportunities to express emotion, not necessarily because they were cynical actors, performing emotion (although some people may have done this on occasion for effect). But rather that the social rules associated with the experience of emotion became naturalised. People are educated from young childhood in appropriate emotional responses and behaviour until it becomes an ingrained activity. Here we might suggest that the 'social' becomes an embodied experience, something the theorist Pierre Bourdieu referred to as 'habitus'.[4] Importantly, this is not the same thing as 'affect', because such emotional responses not only are profoundly shaped by culture but also as this model does not distinguish between emotion that exists before culture and emotion as something we do automatically due to our education.

EMOTION AND THE PAST

When emotions are imagined in this way, a history of emotions becomes important. Understanding how different cultures understood and practised emotion can tell us much about how their societies operated. It also raises a number of interesting questions. One of those questions is: how do emotions change over time? What motivates people to reject their emotional training and respond differently? Like all forms of social deviance (criminality is another good example), why this happens is a topic of considerable debate. William Reddy suggests the idea of 'emotional liberty', where people pursue if not happiness, at least contentment, and so reject emotional rules that come to feel constraining.[5] Why this might happen can be due to changing conditions – the failure of a particular type of economy to enable certain lifestyles for example – or even personal desires, such as same-sex attraction. Or it may be the result of cross-cultural exchange and the opening up of new ways of doing and behaving. For Reddy, our human desire for emotional contentment can drive change.

A history of emotion also raises questions about 'collective' emotion. While acknowledging emotion as learned behaviour highlights its social nature, this is not the same thing as saying that all people in a culture feel the same thing at the same time. Yet, some people wonder whether emotions might be experienced collectively, looking especially at crowd behaviours and emotional contagions.[6] Examples of the latter might include the way that humans often respond to other people's emotions, even when unspoken, so that anxiety can be built and transmitted within a group; or where reporting of a suicide in the press leads to a spike in suicides in the general population. Some scientists talk about this in terms of 'mirroring', people copying other's behaviours and so emotions without realising why. But why this happens remains a topic of considerable debate. If collective emotions remain a contentious idea, that particular societies might be marked by their emotional experience is now recognised in terms like the 'culture of sensibility' to refer to the lauding of emotional expression in eighteenth-century Europe, or the 'age of anxiety' to denote the emotions of the post-9/11 West. Certain emotional norms or concepts might become so culturally significant that they shape the general behaviour of an entire society.

Another key question that arises from thinking about emotions as socially formed is where we place the boundary on emotion. Contagious emotions are suggestive of the idea that our feelings might be transmitted across bodies. But emotions that are informed by society and culture can also be thought of as operating contextually, where the person becomes only one part of an emotional experience. Here we might consider the tiger wandering down a main thoroughfare in New York. How we react to this situation is not just about our personal bodies but our location in a particular physical environment and the cultural ideas and training that inform how we think about tigers, streets and New York. For many historians of emotion, this 'context' becomes critical to emotions, which are not experienced abstractly but in real-life situations.

Thinking about emotions as only 'of the body' misses the way this larger context becomes part of emotional experience, and so part of the definition of emotion itself.

This can be especially important for historians where we have to work with gaps in sources, and especially gaps in narratives of personal experience. If a historian of emotion wants to understand how a particular early modern Indian responded to a tiger in the street, but we have no letters or diaries from that person telling us about this experience, then we have a problem. But we can fill this gap by thinking about how Indians in general understand tigers, emotions and streets, and from this extrapolate an idea of how we might expect this person might have felt in that particular context. This is not perfect of course but part of being a historian involves working with imperfect records, and thinking about individual bodies as only one element in the experience of emotion can highlight the many other dimensions that go into producing our personal experience, some of which are easier to study than what happens inside our heads and hearts.

This way of thinking about emotion could be described as moving our focus from emotions as something 'inside' bodies to something produced socially in relationship with others and the environment. Some theorists, such as Sara Ahmed, have taken this idea further to look at emotions as things that circulate and travel, before 'sticking' in place.[7] Here she is not referring to contagious emotions, but to emotions as things produced by language, and so as conceptual categories that gather additional meanings over time and use. Thus, as different ideas about tigers – as things to fear, as symbols of power, as representations of anger – become more widely known, then tigers become more complex symbols and our responses to them become shaped by these ideas. That we fear a tiger becomes a reaction shaped by the fact that 'fear' has 'stuck' to the tiger, become part of how we understand, and so respond to, tigers. Ahmed particularly reflects on this in relation to categories of people, so that Black people, in her example, become figures of hate, leading to racism as a cultural value. Importantly, emotions that stick to people or things in this context not only help produce our responses to those people or things but can then become deployed in systems of power.

This is a critical idea in the history of emotions, where one of the reasons we care about people's feelings is that they inform how people are treated and whether they are valued, and so can naturalise our justification of wider social systems. If hate sticks to Black people, leading to racism as a social value, then people in that society feel little guilt or concern when refusing Black people full democratic rights, or even placing them in slavery. In contrast, that society might be horrified at the same treatment of a White woman, who is located in the cultural imagination as vulnerable and deserving of care and concern. Emotions, as feelings, direct our responses and behaviour towards various categories of people. As a result, transformations in systems of power require a critical reimagining of not just human rights, but how we feel about people. This makes a history of emotion – a history that interrogates what emotion is and how it became stuck to certain categories of people – vital not just to understanding the past, but to shaping the future.

THE HISTORY OF EMOTIONS

The history of emotion explores how people in the past conceived of, explained and experienced emotions within particular cultures and contexts, with particular attention to variation in experience and to historical change. To understand how historians do this, it can be helpful to think of emotion not just as feeling but as a 360 degree experience that happens in a particular context. Thus, emotion includes the person, what they feel and how they interpret that feeling, but also the location where that feeling happened, the environment, architecture and other people there, and the cultural ideals, values and beliefs about emotion, the body, the individual as a category, and the place where the experience happened. Different emotions historians are interested in exploring different parts of this experience to contribute to a conversation about what emotions are in specific times and places. Historians are also people who have the disadvantage of not being there for the things they study, so they typically have to access this emotional experience through various types of reports, many of which may only capture a small part of this picture.

Many historians like to start with emotion words – things like 'love', 'hate' and 'anger' – and work out what they mean in particular periods. They emphasise not only that different languages have different words for emotion, but that particular emotion words fall in and out of languages over time. They also seek to explore how the same word, say 'anger', might change in meaning over time. For some historians, this is the critical work of the history of emotion as they tie emotional experience quite tightly to language – our job is to identify emotion words and then try to figure out what it meant to feel that emotion (where should one feel it, in what context, and how it was meant to feel). Histories of emotional experience for such historians are expected to flesh out these emotional categories.

Another group of historians, but closely related to the former, are effectively historians of science, medicine or philosophy, and they seek to explore how different cultures understand the experience of emotion as general phenomena. They might highlight, for example, that the medieval passions and affections are not the direct equivalent of modern emotions as they are bound up in theological beliefs about the operation of the soul, rather than biological explanations of the body.[8] Both passions and emotions might be words that explain 'feeling' in the body, but their conceptual basis is quite different. Historians of emotion doing this type of scholarship seek to put the emotion words above into their wider conceptual frameworks, working out how anger might relate to love, or how a society understood the role of emotion in shaping bodies, cognition or ideas of morality.

A third group are interested in exploring emotional experiences. This group can be quite diverse in their approach and method. They are not uninterested in emotion words or the conceptual framework they operate within, things that provide important contexts to interpreting people's experience of emotion. But they are interested in filling some of the other gaps in what an emotion is – where it happens, why and what difference that makes. Sometimes, unlike those interested in emotion words, they study emotional experiences where the emotion in question is not always readily identified. This is not necessarily a study of affect but may just reflect the limitations of the source material. Thus we might look at a set of love letters to explore the romantic relationship between a couple, but nowhere in that set of letters does the word 'love' appear. Indeed, the word 'love' might not occur in that culture, or that particular emotional experience may be described using another word. The historian then has a task of explaining what is going on in this letter without a ready vocabulary to do it, or in the knowledge that they are making a choice to deploy an emotion word to explain what is going on in the absence of direct evidence. They can use the word from that particular culture, justifying this decision from what they know of the uses of the word and the contexts in which they are deployed. They may use the word 'love', from modern English, recognising that it is not a perfect fit but that it most readily conveys what is going on to the modern reader. Here we, the reader of their histories, need to trust that the historian's understanding of that culture is sufficient that they know the correct terms to select to explain the phenomena they are encountering to a modern audience.

One criticism of the latter approach is that it has a tendency to universalise emotional experience. How concerned you are about this might depend on your positioning within the debate around the relationship between materiality and language, and how much agency you give to words in shaping emotional experience, versus other parts of the experience. It may also depend on how universal you believe the human body to be. Some people think that bodies are largely unchanging, so while the words used to explain experience change and those changes add nuance and complexity to our emotional experience, there are some fundamental similarities in human emotional experience, which means we can group certain emotion words together as a single category. *Mēnis, cholos, kotos, orgē* and *thumos* (all Greek), *ira, furor, iracundia, indignatio, stomachari* and *dolor* (in Latin) and *yrre, gram, wod, wroth* and *torn* (in Old and Middle English) may all have slightly different meanings from each other and from the modern word 'anger', but they have enough similarity that we can usefully group them together when exploring the history of anger.[9] If the body is fundamentally similar over time, then these emotion words may also be capturing the same felt experience. Others reject this universalism, emphasising the importance of understanding bodies in context. Yet, even they recognise that there is some overlap in categories that can allow us to use modern English terms to convey these foreign language words to a modern audience. The challenge for the historian here is to use a modern word to convey an old idea, without accidentally bringing a lot of modern 'baggage' to our interpretation of past emotions, or conversely losing some of the nuance of what the original experience incorporated.

One of the advantages of using modern words is that it can direct our attention away from simply the meanings of particular ideas, towards larger conceptual questions about what emotions do in society. If, as Ahmed suggests above, emotions are deployed in systems of power, then we can look at the uses and experiences of emotions as part of the production of social and political relationships, and as implicated in historical change and transformation. Historians whose research focuses on what emotions 'do' are sometimes less concerned about which emotion is doing the work than how our embodied experience of emotion can help us better understand phenomena, like revolutions, riots, shifting moral standards and so forth. This is not to say that they do not care about what emotion is involved in affecting change, but that, as historians working with imperfect and partial sources of evidence, sometimes exploring one part of the question comes at the expense of downplaying another part of the picture.

Historians of emotional experience are also interested in what are sometimes called 'mixed emotions', the idea that categories of emotion (love, hate, anger) only simplistically capture our emotional experience and that we experience complex blends of emotion. Recognising this, particularly when your research interest is in people's emotional experience rather than a particular emotional category, means that attending too closely to particular emotion words can interfere with capturing the richness and diversity of how people live emotional lives, and how their emotions shape the societies of which they are a part. Emotion words become useful conceptual tools for interpreting people's mentalities, behaviours and feelings, but they do not necessarily capture the entirety of either the experience of emotion or how emotions are being deployed in specific situations. Rather as suggested above, the key to understanding emotion is to recognise it as a holistic phenomenon and where historians – human beings with limited time and resources – contribute by exploring particular strands within that phenomenon as part of a group conversation about emotion and its history.

APPLYING EMOTIONS CONCEPTS TO HISTORICAL SOURCES

All historians access the past using historical sources. These can take a wide variety of forms, from letters and diaries, to records produced by institutions, to material culture, to buildings and architecture, even landscape. Most historical sources are made by humans for a particular purpose, and the few that are not are typically made important to historians by the significance that humans placed on them. Traditional source analysis often used the term 'bias' to highlight that the products that survive from the past had their own agendas, and these were often quite different from the agenda of the historian. Today, we prefer the term 'subjectivity' that reflects that the producer and keeper of the source, whether an individual or an institution, had particular interests and intentions in making the source and in enabling its survival over time, so we need to take that into account in understanding and interpreting the source. We also recognise that historians have their own subjectivities, their own cultural influences and personal passions that they bring to their study. This cannot be helped, because, as we explored above, language itself is a cultural product and words bring with them a range of cultural resonances and implications, and so our whole worldview is shaped by our own cultural perspective, as well as our personal identity.

One of the key roles of a historian is to try to interpret a source through the eyes of the society that produced it, and sometimes that which kept a hold of it or used it, whilst also responding to contemporary debates and interests within the field and wider society. The latter is not something that can or should be avoided as historians write history for our present society and to contribute to the concerns of our own age – to give a historical insight into who we are today. An older tradition in research that emphasised 'empiricism', the idea that we should take historical sources at face value, has been largely debunked as we increasingly recognise that language and its uses are not only sensitive to cultural change but also that words can be 'active' in shaping human experience. One of the results of this has been that we now give considerably more attention to expression, word choice and source production than an older generation of historians, who read historical sources for the general picture they provided of a society. An attention to sources as not just carriers of information, but also as material traces of past experience has also heightened the attention we place on the physical source themselves. Thus, a love letter is now read not just for the words on the page, but for ink blots and smudges, for evidence of tears (crying) or wear that suggest it was read multiple times, and interpreted through knowledge of the speed of the post or the likelihood of censorship. The uses of sources become part of their history and so part of how we interpret their meaning.

All of this attention given to the sources has made their analysis more complicated. So has the growth in sub-disciplines within history that focus on particular features or questions about the past. Women's and gender historians, for example, pointed out that much mainstream history ignored women, yet archives were brimming with material about women. Similarly, historians of class and race drew attention to how the presence of Black or working-class historical actors was often ignored in historical scholarship. Emotions historians now make a similar point, arguing that, far from being difficult to find, emotions are everywhere in the archive. If an older generation of historians missed some of these key themes, historians had to ask themselves how such absences might be avoided in the future. Rather than relying on human beings – always flawed – to notice the complexity and breadth of experience that can be found in the archive, we developed or adopted from elsewhere a range of 'concepts', 'methodologies' and even 'theories' to help us work with historical material.

The purpose of these tools was not to complicate the past with modern ideas, but to alert historians to their own biases (reminding them to look for certain things) and to aid us in finding things that were hard to find. Some of these methodologies can be relatively straightforward. The first step in applying gender as a category of historical analysis is just to look for men, women and other gendered categories in your material and to ask what difference gender makes to people's experience in the past. Step two is to look for the absence of particular gender categories from particular records and to 'read against the grain' for what such absences tell us about gender. Step three might become more complicated as you deploy ideas about gendered power to considering the implications of the gendered patterns you have identified for the operation of society. Methodologies for including various groups often work similarly.

Sometimes however methods and theories can be more complicated, requiring analysing historical information through a particular lens of analysis. An example of this might be Pierre Bourdieu's concept of habitus, which argues that many behaviours we consider natural or biological are taught. To apply this method, we often effectively have to go to the record accepting that this is the case and then see whether our material conforms to this interpretation of the world, or whether it challenges that model. Some theories may have steps that need to be followed. Statistical analysis might be a good example here, where you need to shape data according to certain rules to allow you to analyse them numerically.

Importantly, these concepts, methods or theories – words that can sometimes be used interchangeably and sometimes work better in one context than another – are designed to help us maximise the information we can extract from our source material, itself often only small fractions of surviving information about a past society. In an increasingly complex world, where we seek to ask many different sorts of questions from the past, they are also useful for indicating to our readers the boundaries and scope of our study (a shorthand for the assumptions we are making). Thus if we say that we are conducting a gender analysis of a particular set of material, we are not saying that this is the only way such material can be interpreted. Rather we are indicating the approach we are taking, the questions that we wish to answer, and the contribution we wish our scholarship to make. We are also placing 'limits' on our knowledge. Historians only ever contribute a small part to the larger story about the past, and highlighting our boundaries helps direct other historians to where we stopped and what other work is still to be done in the future.

Theories can also be important in helping us not only describe what happened in the past but also explain it. Theory is often particularly important here as it provides models for, say, social change, or the operation of political power, and we can apply those models to our material to explain why things happened in the way that they did. Of course, sometimes models do not align with historical evidence, and this provides historians with an opportunity to refigure old theory or to produce new concepts or methods that can be applied to other material. Unlike scholars in some other fields, for whom theory is applied very exactly as part of their method and often only produced by 'big thinkers', historians are often more relaxed about this process. If it works for our material, we might employ two different theories together or select the parts we find useful. Indeed, sometimes we use ideas because they are 'good to think with' and help us bring a fresh set of eyes to our material, not because we believe that they directly explain what we think is happening. In such instances, theory is working to indicate to our reader how we are thinking about our material and the information we are taking from it, rather than necessarily making larger claims about the nature of our social world.

This book provides an introduction to several key concepts or methods used by historians of emotion to interpret their material and to contribute to our understanding of historical emotions. These are needed because variations not only in language, but also in basic concepts about how bodies work, mean that we cannot simply look for modern words or ideas in the past. They are also important in helping us move from just collecting a group of words that are associated with emotion to understanding how different societies understood, thought about and experienced emotion in a wide range of contexts. Some are particularly useful for contexts where the source material does not contain emotion words, either because they are absent or because they are sources that do not contain writing. Finally, some of the concepts used help us analyse what emotions are doing in society and the role they might play in historical change. This book features many of the main concepts in the field, but there are others available; moreover, in a quickly moving field, there is plenty of space for the historian to expand their theorising of this topic.

CONCLUSION

The history of emotion seeks to understand how emotion is shaped by culture and society, and how this shaping in turn affected social relationships and society. The purpose of the field is to 'denaturalise' a part of human experience that is often assumed to be universal or unchanging. One of the impacts of this is that the language used by emotions historians – affect, feeling, emotion – are not just common-sense terms, but specialist languages that help us explain to our reader what exactly we are talking about in particular historical contexts. Historians of emotion also deploy concepts and methods to their source material to help better denaturalise their material and produce sophisticated analysis of the past. This book provides a range of these methodologies for students to enhance their own research into and interpretation of the past.

FURTHER READING

Using Concepts and Methods in History

Berger, Stefan, Heiko Feldner, and Kevin Passmore, eds. *Writing History: Theory and Practice.* London: Bloomsbury, 2003.

Claus, Peter, and John Marriott. *An Introduction to Theory, Method and Practice.* New York: Routledge, 2012.

Green, Anna, and Kathleen Troup. *The Houses of History: A Critical Reader in Twentieth-Century History*, 2nd ed. Manchester: Manchester University Press, 2016.

Gunn, Simon, and Lucy Faire, eds. *Research Methods for History*. Edinburgh: Edinburgh University Press, 2012.

Howell, Martha C., and Walter Prevenier. *From Reliable Sources: An Introduction to Historical Methods*. Ithaca: Cornell University Press, 2001.

Koselleck, Reinhart. *The Practice of Conceptual History*, trans. Todd Samuel Presner. Stanford: Stanford University Press, 2002.

Salevouris, Michael J., with Conal Furay. *The Methods and Skills of History: A Practical Guide*, 4th ed. Oxford: Wiley Blackwell, 2015.

Tamm, Marek, and Peter Burke, eds. *Debating New Approaches to History*. London: Bloomsbury, 2018.

Tosh, John. *The Pursuit of History: Aims, Methods and New Directions in the Study of History*, 6th ed. London: Routledge, 2015.

Emotions Methodologies

*Broomhall, Susan, ed. *Early Modern Emotions: An Introduction*. London: Routledge, 2016.

*Matt, Susan. 'Recovering the Invisible: Methods for the Historical Study of the Emotions.' In *Doing Emotions History*, eds. Susan Matt and Peter Stearns, 41–53. Urbana: Illinois University Press, 2014.

Reddy, William. 'Against Constructionism: The Historical Ethnography of Emotions.' *Current Anthropology* 38 (1997): 327–52.

Reddy, William. 'The Logic of Action: Indeterminacy, Emotion, and Historical Narrative.' *History & Theory* 40 (2001): 10–33.

Rosenwein, Barbara. 'Theories of Change in the History of Emotions.' In *A History of Emotions, 1200–1800*, ed. Jonas Liliequist, 7–20. London: Pickering and Chatto, 2012.

Rosenwein, Barbara. 'Problems and Methods in the History of Emotions.' *Passions in Context* 1 (2010). www.passionsincontext.de/uploads/media/01_Rosenwein.pdf

Scheer, Monique. 'Are Emotions a Kind of Practice (And Is That What Makes Them Have a History)? A Bourdieuian Approach to Understanding Emotion.' *History & Theory* 51, no. 2 (2012): 190–220.

2 Emotion Words

Emotion words, like 'anger', 'fear' and 'love', play a central role in the history of emotions. As noted in Chap. 1, for some historians identifying such words and then working out what they encapsulate is the key work of the field. Emotion words are also important in helping us understand how humans experience emotion and in figuring out the role of emotion in society. Indeed, a critical idea for historians of emotion is that our feelings are shaped by the language which we use to describe them. Thus, how love is imagined (is it described as a burning fire or sense of contentment?) and the contexts in which it is appropriate (between lovers, or mother and child) shape how we experience that emotion. If love does not feel like a burning fire, then we do not call it love; if love occurs between individuals where it cannot be imagined then we assume the feeling is something else or we do not allow this feeling to exist in the first place. This chapter looks at how historians identify and use emotion words to produce histories of emotion. It begins with a discussion of what emotion words are, why they are important, how we might go about looking for them in source material and what to do with them when we find them. It then provides a case study of the 'love letter', both some background information and sources, that readers can use to try out this technique. The goal is to prepare students to find and use emotion words in other research contexts.

EMOTION WORDS

Words form a critical part of communication in human societies. They categorise both material things, from the human body to objects to people, and abstract ideas, beliefs and values. There are two types of 'emotion words'. The first refers to words that are used to describe particular feelings associated with the body, such as love or anger. The second are words associated with emotional experience, and which help us describe or produce it. These might include 'sensation', 'feeling', 'motion', but could also include words that have rhetorical force in shaping feeling, such as 'child' or 'paedophile'. The first type are more ordinarily associated with the term 'emotion words', but both are important for historians who seek to explore how particular words shape embodied experiences.

When exploring emotion words, it can be helpful to think of a word as a container of associated words, ideas, resonances and materialities. If you were unfamiliar with the word 'love' and asked someone to explain it, they would use another set of associated words to help you get a sense of what it encompassed; they might show you an image or other material representation of it, or describe a context where we might expect love to occur (between a mother and child perhaps). If the word you were uncertain about was associated with an object – like a love letter – they may let you hold and read an example. Thus the meaning of a word is not transparent, but formed through its association with other similar words, relationships, objects and experiences. These associations produce semantic depth and can allow the same word to be used in different situations with varying implications and resonance. Sometimes words come to hold multiple, separate meanings – such as the word 'date' or 'crane' – and their meanings are inferred from their usage. English has a very large vocabulary relative to other languages, and yet most words have multiple uses. This can have interesting effects when the multiple meanings of a term bleed into each other, allowing for jokes and puns but also subtly shaping how each term comes to be understood. It also means there is a considerable degree of 'fuzziness' in human communication, something that is generally considered advantageous when conveying ideas (like emotion) that are abstract or challenging to pin down, but which can cause problems when trying to ensure, for example, that a group of scientists are all thinking exactly the same thing during an experiment.

Importantly for the history of emotions, what a word 'contains' – what is associated with it – can change across different cultures. Love can mean quite different things in the seventeenth century from today, and indeed there is a large literature that tracks these shifting ideas of what is expected from a love relationship.[1] Different times and places also have their own emotional vocabularies. These can include words that describe particular emotional experiences, but also associated terms that form social understandings about how emotions operate or what they do, and emotional words that have rhetorical impact. Some languages have larger vocabularies for emotion than others, and many languages have terms that have no equivalent in other languages, especially as language groups move further apart in their origin. Identifying the words that are associated with emotional experiences is a central task of the history of emotion, and the number of words involved can be surprisingly large and varied.

One of the major challenges of the history of emotions is how to define and translate emotion words for modern audiences. This is especially difficult as it is not just emotion words that change over time. Potentially every word in a historic document might have a different meaning from its modern equivalent (if such an equivalent exists). Learning to 'read' a 'foreign' language, even when that language is the origin of your own language, is a necessary skill for historians, and, like for modern languages, it requires learning new vocabulary, new systems of grammar, and the logical or common-sense structures that shape when words are used and why. Some of this is just about familiarity and simply requires reading widely in the material of the period, with the goal of understanding their language, how they think and use it. But this takes time and is one of the reasons why the study of the past is a skilled practice and why historians tend to get better at interpretation over time.

Once the historian is confident that they understand the language of the period they study, they have the additional challenge of communicating this learning to their audiences, of translating their documents for modern eyes. One advantage of specialist writing, such as we find in journals on particular themes (seventeenth-century history, for example), is that the historian can assume the reader shares some familiarity with the language under question, allowing them to concentrate on explaining new ideas or words. But those aiming for a wider or more general readership have to work harder at explaining their findings. Translating, whether across languages or from the past to the present, is an art, where the word that appears 'equivalent' – 'anger' for *ire*, for example – might distract from the meaning that you wish to get across. Sometimes people use less intuitive vocabularies, or a wider range of describing words, to convey what makes a particular idea distinctive from the modern term. There is no correct way to do this, and indeed the challenges in doing so can lead to debates amongst historians about the best way of explaining a particular term today. Very often we have to be satisfied that we have conveyed the key 'gist' of a conceptual difference to our reader. This is where some of the 'fuzziness' of language can be quite helpful, as sometimes words contain overlap with other words in the associations they 'contain' and this can help us make connections across terms.

APPLYING EMOTION WORDS

If translating emotion across time and place requires patience and attention, there are techniques that historians use to try and make it easier. Many periods contain dictionaries or encyclopaedias that describe common meanings of a particular word. This can be a useful starting place for how a society might define an emotion word (remembering of course that the words used in the definition are also particular to that time period). It is especially helpful if the dictionary/encyclopaedia was written, or updated, around the date that you are studying, as this is more likely to offer a current definition. Many dictionaries are printed repeatedly for many years, and some of their definitions become less relevant over time. Dictionaries are also made by imperfect human beings, and so might reflect the usage of a word amongst a particular group (such as the educated middle classes) but not others. This is especially the case for slang or dialect uses of terms. If a historic dictionary does not survive, a good-quality modern dictionary of etymology can provide a similar function. Here, it is important to select a reliable and scholarly edition, often indicated by the fact that such volumes not only provide a definition but give notes and examples to support their interpretation.

Dictionary definitions offer a useful first step, but this should not be where you stop. Emotion terms take on new meanings and resonances in context and not all of these are captured by the dictionary. Thus it can be useful to trace the word you are interested in over multiple documents, exploring where it was used, what it was trying to convey to the reader or 'do', e.g. is it reassuring someone that they are loved or helping to build anger in a crowd? Once we have mapped where it appears, we can ask particular questions of it. Does this word appear in some types of sources but not others? Does it appear in reference to some forms of relationships, such as marriage, but not others; or in some environments (religious), but not others (political)? Context here can be quite important. It is sometimes tempting to take the writings of philosophers or scientists as definitive as they spend considerable time thinking about emotions and what they are, but their ideas are often experimental or highly-specialist, and do not reflect understanding amongst the general population. In some time periods, it might take a century for scientific ideas to be popularised; in others, they move from one domain to another more quickly. Similarly, some particularly emotional groups of people left fabulous source materials, but their emotional world might be specific to their community or even to them personally. Asking who made it, why and how common these ideas might be provides significant framing for emotional definitions. Once we have answered these questions, we might then ask what these usages suggest about the meaning of an emotion word and the society which is using it in this way.

When doing this, it can be useful to pay attention to what words our emotion word appears alongside. Sometimes the instinct of an emotion's historian is to look for words that appear to explicitly refer to an emotional experience, but this can be at the expense of ignoring other terms that might be strongly associated with emotion within that culture, such as 'heart' for medieval Europeans or 'hormones' today. Thinking about terms that appear in 'emotional contexts' can highlight that a word that we never initially considered to be an emotion word is in fact important to how this community conceptualises the experience of emotion, or may even refer to an emotion itself. We can then take this further by looking at other contexts where this second word was used and using them to build a picture of what both terms mean together. Today, some types of software can help indicate these relationships automatically, but that requires our sources to be digitised and machine-readable, which is not always possible.

Because of the challenges with this work, many historians specialise in particular time periods and the meaning of emotion words in that context. Some however wish to explore how an emotion changed over time, or indeed make comparisons with other places. This can be challenging if you do not have equivalent sources. Comparing variations in the meaning of a word in the dictionary over time might offer a straightforward solution to this problem. But if the sources we have for the medieval period are religious manuscripts and those for the eighteenth century are legal records then we have to be cautious about our comparisons. How do we know if the change we are identifying is an effect of varying ideas or that this emotion was understood differently in religious and legal environments? This is not to suggest that we should not conduct such scholarship; indeed for some periods, the scarcity of source material requires combining materials from quite different times and places to try and develop a picture of society. However it is important to remember that our source material shapes the meanings that we have access to and that how an emotion is expressed in one source does not always capture the fullness of its definition or usage.

As well as exploring emotion words and their meanings, some historians study rhetoric, sometimes defined as 'persuasive writing' but which can be thought of a little more broadly as the use of language to enable certain types of effects on the reader. Rhetoric attends not only to the use and meaning of words, but how they are put together and the deployment of metaphor or other compositional techniques, like hyperbole or alliteration. Most communication is purposeful, that is people speak or write with the intention of doing something. That might simply be to make a connection or express an idea; it may be to give an order or instruction; or describe their research findings to an audience. Quite a lot of rhetoric is designed to convey emotion or to change the emotional state of their audience. Writing within families is often to express love and to maintain affective relationships across distance; here the writer seeks to persuade a reader that the author holds a certain affection for the reader and to encourage them to return such affection, with its associated obligations and duties. A lawyer might use rhetoric to persuade a jury to take their position, asking them to invest in their story. A king might issue a proclamation expressing his anger at his unruly subjects and demanding they reaffirm their loyalty to the crown. Here anger is a threat and through the threat a demand to change one's emotional state.

Historians of emotion that are interested in rhetoric not only explore words that are tightly associated with emotion, like anger or sentiment, but how the emotional resonances that attach to everyday words can be deployed in the production of emotion. The child, for example, has often been used as a motif to provoke sympathy, so that war propaganda – designed to incite a population to fight – may provide stories of children brutally hurt or murdered. This rhetorical effect is possible because 'child' is a word that evokes ideas of innocence and the need for protection, and demands a response from the reader. Some historians are interested in the structure of language, and how things like rhythm or repetition can encourage certain somatic effects in the reader, perhaps encouraging our heartbeat to increase or excitement to grow. Medieval prayers often had a rhythmic quality that was designed to reinforce their meaning and so the spiritual transformation of the person praying. Others again are interested in how word order and use can encourage particular effects on the reader; a play on words might cause someone to laugh or take pleasure in language's slippages.

Understanding the impact of rhetoric can be complicated. Sometimes we have writing manuals or instructional guides, or even critical assessments of writing, that explain how to produce certain emotional effects with words. These can be used to help us understand how a particular culture expected a rhetorical technique to work on their audiences, and so the impact on their emotions. Sometimes we may know how certain texts affected their audiences (such as through news reports or reviews) and can use that to explore which rhetorical forms were producing that emotion. We might have some information about the impact of similar types of material and be able to use that to extrapolate how our text may have been interpreted. Some historians however are willing to accept that some rhetorical techniques might have similar effects today, so that if the pace of a text speeds up that it might have somatic effects on the body that cross cultures and societies. This claim might be based on a belief in the universality of the body, but it might also just acknowledge that some historic cultures are similar to our own, reflecting continuities of ideas and culture.

As I suggest at the beginning, one of the important claims of many emotions historians is that this exploration of words and rhetorical techniques is not disconnected from our embodied experiences. Whilst not everyone will respond as predicted to a rhetorical technique, their effectiveness, and so why they were used, is predicated on the idea that they would have the desired effect at least on some people. Of course, as today, some writers or other producers of rhetoric may have been more talented than others at persuading an audience. But we can usually feel confident that, if we cannot know what happened for a particular individual or at a particular moment, we might know something of how a community responded to such techniques and so how they felt in particular contexts. Emotion words also play an important limiting role on emotion.

They provide the boundaries for how we imagine our emotional lives. If, as we shall discuss in later chapters, some people find that a current model of emotion no longer aligns with their felt experience, it is not necessarily the case that they find alternative modes of expression, perhaps being reduced to confusion or to combining emotion words to try and convey an experience. Indeed, given that so much of our evidence for emotion sees people deploying various emotion words together to develop a broader picture, it may be that a single emotion is often unsatisfactory at capturing what we feel. If this is the case, once we have deployed such words, they can direct us in particular ways – deciding that we are angry may direct us to violence, where irritation may not. Emotion words then play a critical role in not only enabling us to trace change over time in emotional expression, but in how people experienced emotion itself.

WRITING LOVE

The love letter is one of the classic genres of epistolary form, a mode of communication designed to produce connection over distance – whether that was across continents or between bedrooms for warring spouses. Distance is significant to the letter as, unlike emotion expressed in person, it provided space for reflection and consideration of phrase. For those hurt or angry at a beloved, this may have enabled more fruitful communication than the immediacy of fighting in person. For much of history, letters were also delayed in reaching their recipient. Email may be immediate, but even the most efficient postal services took a few hours, many took weeks and months when being conveyed across the globe. Love in this context was produced at a delay; the conversational form of the letter – the back and forth – could be disrupted if one went awry. Once the telegraph was developed, and primarily used for short announcements of bad news, the letter that offered contextual remarks on a depressing telegraph might arrive behind others of a more cheerful sort, leading to odd emotional disjunctures.

Love letters can be found for many historical periods and cultures, especially when we consider the wide array of relationships that could be loving – not just romantic lovers, but families, friends, monarchs and their subjects, gods and their worshippers, and so forth. The eighteenth- and nineteenth-century love letter was produced during a moment where the letter was a prized literary form, found not only in private correspondences, but as a structure for novels and advice writing. The conversational format of the letter – where two or more people are imagined in discussion, and where the imagined recipient plays a central role in shaping the form of the text – provided fruitful opportunity for writers who wished to explain complex ideas, or develop elaborate stories of personal experience. One of the results of this was that letter writers had numerous examples of different genres of letter upon which to model their own writing, not least those provided by letter-writing and etiquette manuals.

Emotion words were critical to the eighteenth- and early-nineteenth-century Anglophone letter, shaped as it was by the culture of sensibility. The latter prized the expression of emotion as key to producing sympathy, a key mode of communication that ensured the ideas transmitted by a writer were understood by the recipient. This encouraged, for a time, the use of particularly overt discussion and expression of emotion, which was thought to give rhetorical force to what was being conveyed. Notably this form of 'flowery' expression could be found in letters between all sorts of people, not just in romantic contexts. Nor were love letters always expected to be private. Courtship letters in particular were expected to be circulated around families; this ensured that men could not be criticised of dishonourable behaviour, protected women from unscrupulous men, and reflected that marriage was still a union of families, not just the couple, and so they had an interest in their love. Letters within marriage sometimes alluded to information that should be kept confidential, but that this was the case is suggestive that many of these letters were also circulated among friends and families. Emotional expression in this context was not considered to be embarrassing or 'private', but a significant language form that evidenced education, emotional intelligence and sophistication.

The use of the language of love also reflected ideas about what love was during the period. Western ideas of love were still closely associated with Christianity, a faith that placed love as a core value. God's love should be channelled by man into their relationships with others, both family and friends, and was often envisioned as quite a passionate affair. As a moral emotion, love was also designed to enforce traditional social hierarchies, so that wives and children showed their love through their obedience to husbands and parents, and the latter in turn exercised an authoritative love without tyranny. Eighteenth-century love was also informed by scientific ideas about natural affection within the family, where love was a 'natural' instinct designed to ensure the successful reproduction of the species. It could be shaped by the nature of the relationship and also those involved. Marital love was often imagined as a union of souls, where female identity was collapsed into that of their husbands. Young love was considered to be hotter and less rational, more likely to lead to rash decisions, but was also admired for its passion. Sex was a significant component of romantic conceptualisations of love, reinforcing the reproductive functions of the household. All or parts of these ideas of love could be drawn on by letter-writers as they communicated their feelings to their reader.

Yet, it was not just words themselves that conveyed emotion. The letter was also a physical item, that could be held, pressed against the body, worn in clothes, carried in pockets, hidden under pillows, and wept over. It was a physical item that could come to stand in place of its author, and so used affectively to aid memory of an absent person or to produce an emotional response in the holder. All of these uses were mentioned in letters, suggesting how descriptions of the use of the letter could also be deployed for rhetorical effect. Writers also indicated emotions in their letters in other ways. An ink spot or shaky hand might suggest the passion or distress of the author (or a bad pen); sketches in the margins could enhance content or communicate alternative messages to those in the text. The type of paper, envelope and postage are useful indicators of social class and wealth, but potentially also of the importance of this letter in the relationship – a proposal of marriage should not be written on a scrap for the social elite, yet the marriage certificates of many poor people were just such material items. The materiality of the letter can be analysed as part of its meaning.

This context shapes how historians approach love letters of the eighteenth and nineteenth century, informing how they analyse them and how they decide what features of the sources they are using are significant or not. This context aids interpretation of the emotion words that they find in their letters, helping them understand what 'love' might mean but also providing an opportunity for them to realise that the emotional expression of the letter they are reading is out of step with the wider culture. A historian may then ask why this is the case and how significant it is to the broader history of emotions during the period. Once they have identified emotion words, worked out the contexts in which they were used, and what they meant, the historian can consider the implications of their findings for a history of love and also for social and emotional relationships of the period. Below are some examples of letters from this period that can be used to apply this technique.

LOVE LETTERS

Love letters were a popular mode of communicating writing in the eighteenth- and nineteenth-century Anglophone world, and can be found between people with a variety of romantic, familial and friendship relationships. Letter-writing and etiquette manuals offered guidance to those composing such work. Letters from this period are full of emotion words. In this section, we shall use some key questions to help us analyse some love letters, drawing on 'emotion words' as a methodological approach. Begin by reading through the examples, getting a sense of their content. Perhaps describe what they are saying in your own words; who is writing to whom, and why are they writing? Then go back to the letters and answer the following questions.

Looking at the letters again, identify the key emotion words. What do they mean? How might we know this and what tools can we use to help interpret their meaning? Can we identify patterns in word usage across letters, people or different groups? What do these patterns, or their absence, suggest? Why are the authors using these words, and what effect do they wish to produce in the reader? Are there other words that reoccur that might have an emotional impact on the reader? Can we count them as 'emotion words'? Are there other techniques being used in these letters to convey emotion or produce it in their reader? Do these techniques increase or reduce the impact of the emotion words used?

Having identified key emotion words, techniques, and their meanings, how might we use them to understand the emotional culture of the writers? Are they particularly expressive, and if so what form does that take? What is the relationship between these emotion words and the emotional experience of the letter writer? Can we know this? What do the emotion words used below tell us of emotional expectations for different relationships in the eighteenth- and nineteenth-century Anglophone world? Can these letters tell us something about romantic love, family life or friendship? What are the limitations of analysing emotion words for understanding the history of emotions? Are there things you could do to make you feel more confident about your interpretation of these letters?

1. Letter-writing manuals

The Complete Letter-Writer, containing Familiar Letters on the Most Common Occasions in life (Edinburgh, 1789) was a manual that offered exemplar letters for people to model in their writing.

> From a young lady to her papa, who lately embarked for the East Indies, in the Company's service, but was detained at Portsmouth by contrary winds
>
> Dear Pappa,
>
> I flatter myself you are too well convinced of my steady adherence to my duty and affection, ever to imagine I will omit the least opportunity that offers to pay you my humble duty.
> I beg my dear papa may not be offended if I say, that it gives me secret satisfaction to hear you are still within the reach of a post-letter; and though I cannot have the pleasure of a paternal embrace, yet I rejoice in the expectation of receiving the wished for account of your health's continuance, which to me, my dear mamma, and brother, is the greatest blessing that Providence can possibly bestow upon us.
> Oh! Sir, tho' short to some, the interval of time since I received your blessing, ere your departure from us, to me it seems an age! And when

I reflect how many more I am doomed to bear in the absence of the best of parents, I am inconsolable! And if it were possible that nature could subsist on sleep alone, I could with pleasure renounce every amusement whatever, and make the silent pillow my retreat.[2]

From a sailor to his sweetheart

My deary Peggy,

If you think of me half so often as I do of you, it will be every hour; for you are never out of my thoughts; and when I am asleep, I constantly dream of my dear Peggy. I wear myself a bit of gold always at my heart, tyed to a blue ribbon round my neck; for true blue, my dearest love, is a colour of colours to me. Where, my dearest, do you put yours? I hope you are careful of it: for it would be a bad omen to lose it.

I hope you hold in the same mind still, my dear; for God will never bless you if you break the vows you have made. As to your ever faithful William, I would sooner have my heart torn from my breast than it should harbour a wish for any other woman besides my Peggy. O, my dearest love! you are the joy of my life! my thoughts are all of you; you are with me in all I do; and my hopes and my wishes are only to be yours.[3]

2. *Letters between courting couples and within marriage*

Romantic letters are often the most familiar to modern audiences. Below are some eighteenth-century examples. Mary Hutton was the mistress of Gilbert Innes of Stowe, a Scottish banker, for over a decade. He refused to marry her, and their sexual relationship ruined her reputation, causing her significant social isolation and economic marginalisation after their affair was made public. The letter below is from several years into their relationship. The second letter in this section is between the Rev. Philip Doddridge and his wife Mercy, relatively early in their married life. Doddridge was a well-known English minister and advice writer. They eventually had nine children.

Mary Hutton to Gilbert Innes of Stowe

Glasgow 7th Apr 1825

My Dear Monsieur

I am become anxious to hear from you and it is a fortnight past this evening since I saw you & your promises that Evening were very gratifying to me You promised readily to write me often and also said you would be better and kinder to me then you was last year. Yet a fortnight is past cruel Monsieur and I have never heard whether you are well or not. I told you that I was very unwell – and my feet continues so much swelled that I have not got on a shoe since I saw you except a new pair which is nearly ½ an inch every way larger then even the large shoes that I used to wear for my sore toes. This is the way I have laid out the £5 you gave me for Clothes. A gown £2.2 Bonnet £2.4 shoes 7/ gloves 2/ materials for corsets which I am to make myself 8/6 I have written to Miss Porteous Crieff – that if convenient I am coming to pay them a visit but have not got an answer yet should she accept of me. I have planned to stay 2 weeks which will just about pay my expenses going & returning but as I am very Bare of cloaths. I hope you will let me get a few things more to appear decent otherways I will not go at all Look my Dear Monsieur at what I will want a Gown about £3.3 three shifts which I will make myself £1-1 a pr of fine shoes 9/ silk stockings perhaps 9/ or 10 two caps £1-1 two pr of gloves 4/6 sundries such as ribbons, frills & £1 O! my dear monsieur approve of this – if they really accept of my bind which I will inform you of as soon as I get an answer from Crieff. You never believe me that I manage very frugally and when I tell you that I have often wanted my dinner to save money I almost believe you think it a downright lie but my dear Monsieur You do not look at the particulars of my life Wd every one know that it is expensive living from Home Ah! Remember that I have been from home these 11 years for instance when I come to Glasgow I did not got my lodgings till the Wednesday following, where could I go but to an Inn & I went to the cheapest at Port Dundas And I payed for four nights lodging & my breakfast four times, which came to 12/ & a shilling for cleaning my shoes but had I taken dinner, tea and supper I would have had a very different bill to pay. I left the Inn always about 11 oclock & wandered about the town & rested myself in shops upon a glass of whisky & some gingerbread till 10 oclock at night when I returned to the Inn to my Bed. She is an old cankered Body I live with but she is honester then most of her kind Her Rooms are 12/ a week including fire & Bed & Table linen which is reasonable considering the way Rooms let in Glasgow. My dear Monsieur I hop of you to write me a few lines And I always am yours affectionately &&&[4]

Philip Doddridge to Mercy Maris Doddridge

16 Jul 1734, Hackney

My Dearest Creature can hardly imagine the Pleasure with which I receiv'd hers for which indeed I had waited with some Impatience I am very much oblig'd to you for the great Care & Tenderness which you express on my Account & assure you my Love, I will be so just to you as to take all possible Care of my self. My Friend here & especially those of Mr Waters's Family treat me in the most engaging Manner I can truly say I never met with greater Kindness in any Journey I ever made. As for Hurry & Fatigue tho some Degree of it be unavoidable yet I make it as moderate as possible by allowing my self all proper Assistances from Water men & Hackney Coaches. Yesterday I dined wh Mrs Cooke & to Day I wait upon My Lady Russell who was to be in Town on Thursday. And the beginning of next Week I propose going to Ongar. Abundant friends enquire after you & send Service to you especially those of this family whose remarkable & most endearing goodness to me I desire you would take some Notice of in your next. Mr Waters who is undoubtedly one of the best of Men seldom fails to pray very particularly for you when he officiates in the Family & his pretty Daughter tells me that a Thousand kind things she does for me are for your sake. In short my Dear I know not when I shall have an Opportunity of making you a greater Compliment or rather of giving you a greater proof of my sincere & tender Affection than when I tell you that you are so dear to me that your Absence is a very sensible Affliction to me even here. I have the pleasure to think that I shall have you in my Arms in less than a Fortnight and in the Mean Time would never forget her at the Throne of Grace who has so great an Interest there & so constantly employs it for me. My hearty Service attends all Friends assure Mrs Wright that I don't forget her & hope amongst all my Friends some thing may be done towards obtaining her a Comfortable Settlement where the Necessity of our Affairs must oblige us to resign the pleasure of her Company & Assistance. As for the House do as you please. I hear at present of no more Pupils. I depend upon it that Mr Hawtyn & Mr Wilkinson will take Care of Jacky of yr ingenious Mr Hextall. Assure Jacky that I shall be greatly disappointed if he be not very perfect in all the Greek Vers both Active & Passive Barytones & Circumflexes. I don't trouble him wt more particular Directions knowing under whose Direction she is. Mr Waters & his Lady, Nr J Waters & his Sister join their Services to you. She is for the Fair Lady I mentioned last she is so fast asleep that I do not apprehend her at present capable of servicing you which however she will certainly do before night in entertaining me. Yet after all my Dear there is no Entertainment so delightful to me as that wh you Letters give me wh there fore I hope you will be so good as to continue & frequently my Dearest Self yours most obliged faithful & affect. Servt Doddridge.

I have a key in my pocket wh I suspect to be that of your Chest of Drawers preay forgive my stealing it thro' the Goodness of God
Since I wrote I've rece'd Mr Hawtyns & heartily thank him for the Care he has taken of my people & of you I desire he would continue his Lectures in the parlour. Now I mention Mr Hawtyn desire him to give my hearty service to Miss Roppit & wh it what else he pleases in my Name. I hope the Elbow will be kept down.[5]

3. *Letters of friendship*

It was not just families that wrote affectionately to each other. Below are the letters of Daniel Webster to various male friends. Webster was a Boston lawyer, who later became a senator. These letters are from his early life, when studying law and trying to establish his career.

Daniel Webster to George Herbert

Dartmouth College, December 20, 1798

Yes, George, I go, I leave the friends I love,
Long since 'twas written in the books above;
But what, Good God! I leave thee, do I say?
The thought distracts my soul and fills me with dismay.
But Heaven decreed it, let me now repine;
I go; but, George, my heart is knit with thine.
In vain old Time shall all his forces prove,
To tear my heart from the dear friend I love.[6]

Daniel Webster to James Hervey Bingham

Salisbury, February 11, 1800

Brother Bingham, – I now sit down in poor spirits to write a poor letter, to – a poor fellow, shall I say? No, say rather, to the friend of my heart, the partner of my joys, griefs, and affections, the only participator in my most secret thoughts. I arrived here yesterday, seasonably for school, and having undergone the fatigues of the day, I retired to rest at nine o'clock and surrendered myself to the dominion of Morpheus. At then I was awaked, and informed that Captain McClure and Senior Curtis were below. I soon disengaged myself from the 'slumbering god,' and hastened to extend them the friendly right hand, accompanied with a hearty how do you do! They left Hanover almost two weeks since; and have taken a tour of the southeast. By them I was favoured with two letters from our friends at college, which, although dated some time ago, gave me much pleasure. Clark writes that he had taken the school there at twenty-four dollars per month. Doctor Marsh offered himself for fifteen, but was not received. 'This,' Clark observes, 'feeds my vanity, but not my purse.' In the course of his letter he observes, 'blow ye Northern blasts with tenfold fury; beat back the pestilential breeze of matrimony or my Icarus is fallen forever!' What does he hint at here? How should he know that I was just about to (try to) be married? My amour, you very well know, had not commenced the last time I wrote to him. He says he is well and happy; that he has heard from many of our friends who are in health. This information carries joy to the hearts of J.H.B and D.W. While you rejoice with me in the health and happiness of our brother students, I presume from the goodness of your heart, that you will join me in commiserating him with stands next to yourself on the catalogue of my friends. I mean Bracket; he has lost a sister; he is afflicted, and we will mourn. We have seen him in those happy hours, when every heart palpitated with joy, and every eye sparked with benevolence; and we should be equally happy to meet him now and mingle souls in mournful sympathy. [Discusses the deceased's qualities, before moving on to gossip attached to other friends, and the content of a previous letter] It is now nine o'clock; before I began this letter I read a chapter in Mallet du Pain's History of the Destruction of the Helvetic Union. I read till I saw Switzerland ravaged and depopulated, her sons barbarously butchered, and blood flowing in torrents from the side of the Alps! All this I saw done by the intrigue of perfidious France. The scene was too affecting; I closed the book and exclaimed, 'Havoc and spoil and ruin are thy gains; destruction is they sport; blood groans, and desolation are they triumphs, thou magnanimous republic!!! [Discusses this history in detail, before quoting a related poem] I am Sir, with much respect, yours in the indissoluble bonds of fraternal love, Dan. Webster.[7]

Daniel Webster to James Hervey Bingham

Salisbury, February 22, 1803

My good Hervey – Yours of January 29, was received in due season. I thank you for the expressions of friendship it contained, and for the assurance that a part of your time is devoted to me. At this period of our acquaintance I need not tell you what pleasure I receive from your letters, nor with what exultation my heart glows under the impression that our early congenial attachments will never be sundered. It may look a little like vanity, flattery, and puerility, but I think I may say that you will continue to occupy the parlor of my affections, till Madam comes! Madam, you know, must have the parlor, but even then you shall not be cast off into the kitchen. Depend on it, if Madam treats you, or anybody else who is an older proprietor than herself, with prankish airs, we will soon away with her.[8]

Daniel Webster to James Hervey Bingham

Salisbury, December 23, 1803

Dear Hervey – I cannot say that your last arrived as soon as I looked for it; for I am always looking for your letters; but I had it as soon as I had a right to expect it. Frequent letters are not, perhaps, absolutely essential to friendship; but they are the best and most natural consequence of it. You and I should certainly always be friends, if we never wrote another syllable to each other; but we should be friends to little purpose, if we never mutually contributed any thing to soften care and cheer the heart. Your letters have become a settled portion of my happiness; the force of habit is added to the force of esteem, and if you should intermit writing for a long time, there would be a kind of vacuum in my pleasures that I could not handily fill with anything else.[9]

CONCLUSION

Eighteenth- and nineteenth-century letter writers, especially of the educated middle classes, were often remarkably self-conscious in the production of the love letter. These were artistic works that not only expressed how they felt but were expected to deploy elegant terms and elaborate language to do so. Such art might especially be found at the beginning or end of letters, whilst the content could cover more pedestrian or everyday ground. Yet, even here, many writers chose topics that enhanced the intimacy between reader and writer, discussing mutual friends or family, the operation of the household, or even like Mary Hutton, using an account of her purchases to bring her lover into her production of an imagined 'home' together, where she was a frugal wife and he a generous provider. Many described imagined physical encounters, such as an embrace, or gifts that could be held and felt as a replacement for the absent beloved.

These techniques for producing emotion were taught to this social group through writing manuals, and as they were encouraged to write letters from childhood so had read many examples over their lives. Yet, these techniques were not expected to reduce the emotional 'authenticity' of the expression, but to provide people with a language and skillset for conveying how they felt effectively in the form of the letter. The time and labour that went into producing some of these letters are suggestive that 'art' itself might be a useful measure of affection, a demonstration to the reader that the writer cared enough to take time and care in the production of a source designed to show their love.

Emotion words were a critical part of producing affection through the love letter, providing a language – 'affection', 'pleasure', 'love' and 'joy' – to convey love and how it should be felt. These terms, and their combined usages, are suggestive of how emotion words came as part of conceptual clusters that together shaped each other's meaning and of the expected repertoire of feeling when experiencing love in various forms. They provide the historian a key entry point into the emotional experience of this social group and the mechanisms that they used to manage their love relationships. How love might be expressed, and the domain of feeling it was associated with, changed over time. Yet, emotion words can provide a fruitful access point to tracking such shifts, as well as offering insight into a wide domain of other emotional experiences.

FURTHER READING

Emotion Words

*Boddice, Rob. *The History of Emotions*, 41–58. Manchester: Manchester University Press, 2018.

*Frevert, Ute. 'Defining Emotions: Concepts and Debates over Three Centuries.' In *Emotional Lexicons: Continuity & Change in the Vocabulary of Feeling 1700–2000*, eds. Ute Frevert et al., 1–31. Oxford: Oxford University Press, 2014.

Rosenwein, Barbara. *Emotional Communities in the Early Middle Ages*. Ithaca: Cornell University Press, 2011.

White, R. S. 'Language of Emotions.' In *Early Modern Emotions: An Introduction*, ed. Susan Broomhall, 33–6. London: Routledge, 2017.

Wierzbicka, Anna. '"Happiness" in Cross-Linguistic and Cross-Cultural Perspective.' *Daedalus* 133 (2004): 34–43.

Wierzbicka, Anna. '"History of Emotions' and the Future of Emotion Research.' *Emotion Review* 2 (2010): 269–73.

Love Letters

Barclay, Katie. *Love, Intimacy and Power: Marriage and Patriarchy in Scotland, 1650–1850*. Manchester: Manchester University Press, 2011.

Barclay, Katie. 'Marginal Households and their Emotions: The 'Kept Mistress' in Enlightenment Edinburgh.' In *Spaces for Feeling: Emotions and Sociabilities in Britain, 1650–1850*, ed. Susan Broomhall, 95–111. London: Routledge, 2015.

Barnes, Diana G. 'Emotional Debris in Early Modern Letters.' In *Feeling Things: Objects and Emotions Through History*, ed. Stephanie Downes, Sally Holloway and Sarah Randles, 114–32. Oxford: Oxford University Press, 2018.

Bound, Fay. 'Writing the Self? Love and the Letter in England, c.1660–1760.' *Literature and History* 11, no. 1 (2002): 1–9.

Brant, Clare. *Eighteenth-Century Letters and British Culture*. Basingstoke: Palgrave Macmillan, 2006.

Earle, Rebecca. 'Letters and Love in Colonial Spanish America.' *Americas* 62, no. 1 (2005): 17–46.

Godbeer, Richard. *The Overflowing of Friendship: Love Between Men and the Creation of the American Republic*. Baltimore: John Hopkins University Press, 2009.

Harris, Amy. 'This I Beg My Aunt May Not Know: Young Letter-Writers in Eighteenth-Century England, Peer Correspondence in a Hierarchical World.' *Journal of the History of Childhood and Youth* 2, no. 3 (2009): 333–60.

Jensen, Katharine Ann. *Writing Love: Letters, Women and the Novel in France, 1605–1776*. Carbondale and Edwardsville: Southern Illinois University Press, 1995.

Lyons, Martyn. 'Love Letters and Writing Practices: On *Ecritures Intimes* in the Nineteenth Century.' *Journal of Family History* 24 (1999): 232–39.

Lyons, Martyn. '"Questo cor che tuo si rese": The Private and the Public in Italian Women's Love Letters in the Long Nineteenth Century.' *Modern Italy* 19, no. 4 (2014): 355–68.

Redford, Bruce. *The Converse of the Pen: Acts of Intimacy in the Eighteenth-Century Familiar Letter*. Chicago: Chicago University Press, 1986.

3 Styles

Emotional styles were an idea first realised in the work of Carol Stearns and Peter Stearns, and have been significant for many scholars researching the history of emotion. It is a concept that contributes to one of the key debates in the field around the 'gap' between language and personal experience, and especially between social norms and the individual. Particularly for Peter Stearns, the concept was important in allowing historians to explore change over time in ideas about emotion, and to map emotions onto specific 'generations' or historical periods. Stearns and Stearns used the word 'emotionology' to describe the study of emotional styles. This chapter introduces the concept of emotional styles and how historians might go about looking for it in their source material. It has a particular focus on how we might identify styles of emotion in visual imagery, and so uses a case study of the history of tears in art across time and culture. A history of tears offers a distinctive history of a bodily action associated with emotion, but where there is significant cultural variation in when displaying tears was appropriate, for whom, and what they meant.

EMOTIONAL STYLES

An emotional style can be loosely thought of as similar to other forms of 'fashionable styles,' although generally less rapidly changed or individually personalised. Here we might consider a 'goth' of the 1980s and early 1990s, typically a young person who wore a lot of black, dark or black/white contrasting make-up, dark hair, and who enjoyed a particular range of post-punk rock music; they were generally associated with a 'low-energy' emotional style, little smiling or enthusiasm, sometimes depression and self-harm. There was also some variation within the culture, with some groups rejecting drugs and violence for reading and poetry. Goths had a distinctive aesthetic, that ranged across and incorporated their emotional experience and how they displayed their emotions to others.

Like many forms of style, identifying the boundary between 'performance' and 'identity' for goths is challenging. On the one hand, this was a subculture whose style was reliant on a particular aesthetic performance – they wore specific and distinctive clothes, heavy makeup, dyed their hair – that could be discarded if they decided to leave that culture. On the other hand, most, perhaps all goths, saw this aesthetic performance as a central mechanism for conveying their 'self' to others and in producing community. That they required 'props' to enable this presentation of self did not make it less 'authentic' or 'genuine' than other forms of self expression. Rather that their cultural expression was at odds with mainstream expressions of identity merely acted to denaturalise identity and selfhood for everybody and to reinforce its performative dimensions.

Emotional styles can be considered in a similar way, as trend or fashion in emotional expression and experience. Stearns and Stearns argued that an emotional style was the 'attitudes or standards' that a society or group held about 'basic emotions', their appropriate expression, how they encouraged or maintained that expression through institutions or education, and the daily behaviour that enforced that emotional expression.[1] An example might be that anger should not be expressed by women, so that female anger was disapproved of, women were taught through advice literature or childhood discipline not to express anger, and that when they did people might shun them or shake their heads disapprovingly. An emotion style, however, was more than just a cultural attitude towards a single emotion, but rather an entire cultural framework that organised emotional life either for a whole society or for a subculture within it. Peter Stearns wrote about 'American cool' as a style of emotion that encouraged a general aversion to 'intense' emotions, discouraging people from overt or passionate emotional expression across their entire lives, both in private and public contexts.[2] In contrast, the eighteenth-century culture of sensibility reified such expression, encouraging and lauding emotional outbursts.

One of the key elements of Stearns and Stearns' imagining of emotional style is the concept of 'basic emotions', that underneath culture there is a set of emotions that are broadly shared across time and space, and which they manage and give shape through cultural expression. A key principle of the concept of style is that there is a gap between culture and the body that has to be managed. This can allow considerable space within a society for people to contest or reject the emotional 'style' of the mainstream and develop subcultures, or alternatively to try and fail to live up to the ideal (for example, by being too emotional in a 'cool' society). Theorists since Stearns and Stearns have been less worried about whether the underpinning emotions in this theory are 'basic' in the sense of being universal, but still find it a useful idea for exploring how cultures try to shape and manage the emotions of people.

For later emotions scholars, a gap may arise between culture and individual expression because there can be considerable variation and contest in society about how emotions should be expressed, and especially how they should be expressed in particular contexts. They point, for example, to the way that the permitted emotional behaviour at a sports ground might be quite different from that allowed in the workplace, and that middle-class people might have a different emotional style than working-class people, leading to problems for those who move across social classes. In the same way that a goth might have to reduce their makeup, wear a uniform, and be cheerful at work, so people might need to reframe their emotional style for different environments.

One of the questions that arise from this is the place of 'authentic' emotional expression within a particular style community, where authentic is not necessarily a reference to basic emotions but to behaviour which a person performs unthinkingly. Some, like Arlie Hochschild who looked at how air hostesses were taught to be always calm and cheerful, argue that emotional performances for new contexts begin as a form of work (we need to think about it and remember to do it), but that over time, this emotional behaviour becomes 'naturalised', a learned behaviour that we do unthinkingly.[3] An inexperienced goth might feel self-conscious about their new aesthetic, but eventually not give it a second thought when out in public. Emotional styles might also be taught in a 'naturalised' fashion so that people learn to emote differently for different audiences from childhood and so are not aware of this shifting across repertoires of expression when they move across environments. Yet, if emotional styles can be naturalised, part of their usefulness as a concept for historians is that they are not a form of 'habitus', as Bourdieu would describe it (that is, they are not embodied habits learned from childhood). Rather it is the possibility that emotional styles can be taken up and put down – just as being a goth can be taken up and then left behind – that makes them helpful for historians.

Emotional styles allow historians to think about the way that societies provide rules for emotional behaviour that individuals do not always conform to and to think about why this is the case. This is similar to other studies of 'deviance' and 'subcultures' that seek to understand why individuals and groups are different and how such difference emerges within societies. Emotional styles therefore allow us to look at how individuals mediate their own experience of emotion within wider group norms. Studying emotional styles also allows us to think about power, asking why certain forms of emotional expression become dominant and how this prioritising of emotional expression can act to give power to those that conform and to exclude those that do not. Emotional styles are also useful because they allow us to group emotions like anger or hate together to think about emotion as a broader phenomenon in a society, a 'style' for a particular group. This can be helpful in thinking about emotions at the level of society, rather than the individual, and for making comparisons between different societies and time periods; it gives us some large conceptual categories for comparative purposes without getting lost in all of the detail and complexity of individual experience. Styles are sometimes seen as more useful than ideas like 'habitus' as they are more fluid and more easily associated with specific environments, rather than innate behaviours.

APPLYING EMOTIONAL STYLES

Emotional styles consist of (1) rules for the expression of emotion and how they are enforced through institutions or group norms; (2) the way that people perform those rules through their bodily expressions, gestures, behaviour and dress, and ideally personal feelings; (3) the physical contexts where these emotional rules apply (the workplace; twentieth-century America). Styles consist of 'common scripts', or a general set of rules that give broad shape to the style, and the way that these rules are given shape by individuals within particular contexts. Whilst goths might be defined by a general set of features that identify them as a group, an individual goth has some autonomy in how they dress, wear their make-up, and choice of favourite song, that allows them to personalise that style to express an identity that is both individual but reflective of group norms. The historian can access styles in two ways. First they may look for sources that give them access to the 'general rules' for a group; or they can look at individual behaviours and try to identify patterns that conform to a style. Here the context in which particular emotional expressions happen can be especially important.

The early work on emotional styles focused on prescriptive and advice literature, the self-help manuals, etiquette guides and training manuals for workplaces, that set out expectations for how to behave in general society and in specific environments. They sought to identify particular emotion words like 'anger' and then to explore the guidance offered to people on when and where to express anger, how it should be done, and where it was not appropriate. Nineteenth-century elite men were not supposed to express anger in public, but if they did they should control their temper and deportment, not offering violence. Men who became red-faced, loud or belligerent were then seen as unmanly. Advice books helped advise men on these rules so they could learn to express or repress anger in 'manly' ways.

It can be tempting to see such prescriptive literature as the 'rules' for a culture and the way people behave as conforming or not to these rules. But in practice, emotional rules are the things societies produce as a group, and advice books are just one corner of that. They may contain quite idiosyncratic perspectives, reflecting the author's own opinion or specialist training; they may be aspirational, as when self-help gurus try to teach us to behave more healthily. They may be trying to shape cultural behaviour, such as when parenting manuals advise parents not to spank their children, but not reflective of practice or even mainstream beliefs. The historian then has to approach such advice carefully, exploring where it came from and why it was written. At the same time, because such books are products of the culture that produced them, they do tell us something of wider cultural norms and values, even if not always what the author might have anticipated.

Popular culture, like songs, plays, novels and later television, is also a useful resource for exploring questions of style. They not only give us 'ideal' rules but examples of people who break those rules and how they should be treated. Here we might see depicted an angry man, with his red face and blustering behaviour, and notice that people shook their heads or disapproved. We thus learn not only what anger should look like, but also how people were expected to respond. A similar picture can also be built from sources about real lives, whether that is descriptions in newspapers about events or even analysing the expression of love in a love letter as a form of 'style'. Here we might be especially interested in how people are applying these rules in practice (or not). If this is our only type of source, we may want to look at many similar examples so that we can build a bigger pattern of behaviour for a society, and not just the individual. This often means attending to similarity and difference and trying to construct the rules by ourselves through looking for common patterns.

One interesting component of emotional styles is recognising that breaking the rules might also form part of a cultural style. Thus men might be educated that expressing anger is unmanly, but if they are given lots of ideas about what anger might look like – red faced, blustering, aggression – then they are also being taught how to express anger. We can then suggest that sometimes emotional styles consist of both 'good' emotional behaviour and 'bad' emotional behaviour, but that both come together to shape the overall style of a culture. This might be because that culture imagines emotion as a bodily force, trying to burst out, and that emotional rules are there to help people control that. Thus we might say that the emotional 'style' of that culture is a 'hydraulic model' where people are trying to manage an underlying natural force. This might be quite different from a society that does not see emotions as so energetic and in need of such management.

Because emotional styles focus on emotional rules and their expression, a considerable focus of historical interest is on the external display of emotion. This means exploring physical descriptions of the body and especially the face – do they smile or cry; do they change colour – and how the body behaves – does a person retreat behind a rock or punch the person next to them? We might also be interested in clothing and appearance, both because it might be associated with an emotional subculture (like goths and their 'low energy' expression) or particular rituals related to an emotion, like wearing black or shaving one's head when in mourning. These forms of expression become an important part of understanding the style of an emotional culture. Because of this, visual sources, including paintings, prints, film and television, can be useful as they sometimes depict people showing emotion or doing activities associated with emotion (such as crying or laughing). Such images allow us to consider what emotion 'looked like' to other people in that culture and how they may have identified emotion when they saw it expressed by other people. We can compare different images of people expressing the same emotion, or conversely physical gesture, and try to assess what the social rules were for conveying that emotion.

Looking for emotional styles therefore involves collecting either a large set of the same source or an array of different sources for a particular culture or subculture, and then charting similarities and differences in both emotion rules and in the expression of emotion by individuals. Like with our search for emotion words, sometimes emotions are signalled directly ('anger should be contained') but sometimes it can be less direct, so that advice to women to remain quiet when around men might also be interpreted as a form of emotion management. When looking at multiple images of funerals, we might notice that women are often depicted holding handkerchiefs to their face and come to recognise that this was a common representation of grief, which tells us something of how people should express grief in that culture. As an emotional style not only refers to how we manage one emotion, but a general cultural trend in emotion management, it is also important to consider more than one type of emotion. Therefore we may wish to combine a study of grief, with anger and love, and to consider what these different expressions have in common or not. Thus, for Stearns 'American cool' meant that all forms of emotional expression should be restrained and tightly managed. But in some cultures, there may be considerable space to express grief, but not to show anger. Working out the 'logic' that underpins these decisions may help us interpret an emotional style as a broader set of general rules; at times this may not be possible and all we can do is describe how an emotional style was performed by a particular culture in a certain environment.

TEARS IN HISTORICAL CONTEXT

Today, we often associate tears particularly with grief, but if we stopped and thought for a moment we might also remember experiencing tears of joy or laughter, perhaps even of frustration. Tears are a particularly interesting motif or symbol, as they appear in many cultures but what they 'signify' (or mean) is not always the same. Much of the time, they appear to be associated with the expression of emotion or other forms of embodied experience, such as pain or being overwhelmed. Indeed, if many bodily expressions – from facial gestures to temperature or physical behaviour – can be ambiguous to audiences when viewed out of context, tears might at least provide an indicator that something emotional is happening, if not what. Source materials that display or describe tears, or associated phenomena like weeping, can then be a useful starting point for historians of emotions. Like an emotion word, they might act as a sign that something emotional is happening and allow us to begin unpacking what that might be. How a community treats tears in particular contexts – whether they hide them beneath a handkerchief or display them proudly in public spaces – can also help us start to understand about emotional styles, of how, when and in what form people are permitted to express specific emotions.

There has been quite a lot of research on the history of tears because of their importance as an emotional symbol. People have investigated the contexts in which people weep. Crying before pieces of art is especially interesting as it seems to evidence of the capacity of art to 'move' people, without necessarily directing people to a specific emotion, like grief or happiness. Tears also feature in art, especially in religious contexts. Here tears are both used as a physical evidence of what the person being portrayed is feeling and are designed to encourage the same or a similar feeling in a viewer. Much religious art was used as part of devotional practices, so that people considered what they were seeing and used such imagery to direct their own emotions accordingly. Appropriate emotional responses to devotional art could aid Christians to be brought closer to God. Tears in art have also been used to provide a wide array of messages to audiences. Monarchs sometimes used tears as part of visual expressions of anger or disappointment that were expected to encourage reform in their unruly populations. Viewing tears was expected to direct the feelings of the watcher, either by directing them to similar feeling or by encouraging them to consider the causes of tears.

Tears could also operate similarly in everyday contexts. Irish judges sometimes wept in courtrooms in the early nineteenth century when making death penalty pronouncements. Tears here were associated with sympathy and emotional depth; they allowed judges to indicate to audiences that such decisions were not made 'unfeelingly' and so to convince them that justice was served. Many reports note that weeping judges could shape the emotional tenor of the room, encouraging the court gallery to weep with them. In this way, weeping could be contagious. Importantly, as the Irish public was not always in agreement with the decisions of the court, it was a way of neutralising potential violence at these decisions. Weeping allowed an emotional outlet for the emotions in the court, directing them away from anger or violence.

If tears perform important work in helping historians identify that emotion is present, as the last example suggests they also start to help us explore the idea of emotional style. That weeping in Ireland was viewed positively and could be used to create a sympathetic exchange between the weeper and their audience suggests something of Ireland's appreciation for sentimental behaviour and their valuing it as an authentic expression of self. Thomas Dixon used this idea to build a picture of Britain's changing emotional styles from the medieval period onwards, arguing that studying weeping and attitudes towards it could be used to build a picture of a culture's varying emotional styles over time and so offered us the capacity to track such change.[4] Below are a number of examples of images of weeping across time and different cultures.

REPRESENTING TEARS

As a symbol, tears and weeping have been deployed by a variety of different cultures to depict emotion and to make political or moral points. Below is a selection of visual representations of weeping in Europe and Asia. How might we interpret these images as historians of emotion? Begin by looking at the images below and describing what you see. What does each picture include – people, animals, clothing, props, physical environment? What sorts of body gestures or facial expressions are represented? Is the image telling a particular story, or providing a message? How does each part of the picture contribute to its message? Are there competing messages in the same image? How do we know this – is it something about the people, props, their emotions or something else? What difference does the material – a painting, a print, a ceramic – make to the meaning of the image? What about the usage of these images by the cultures that produced them – do we know what they were used for and by whom? How does this usage shape how we might interpret the image? How important is knowledge of wider context of the place and period to interpreting these images? Are there any universal features that are notable across these examples?

Having asked these questions, we can then ask what we might learn about both tears and the 'emotional style' of a particular culture. How are tears displayed in these images? Are tears always represented in the same way? How does the representation of tears relate to other bodily gestures or appearances; does this help us interpret the tears? Who is weeping, and who is not? What might be the cause of such tears, and their absence in others? How do we know that from the image or its uses? What do these images tell us about the appropriateness or not of weeping in particular times and places? Can we deduce from them whether crying is valued positively or not? Can we learn about whether weeping is associated with particular emotions – sadness, joy? Can we take these findings further to reflect on what that might tell us about these cultures' relationship to expressing emotion in general? Are there any limitations to using these sorts of sources for interpreting emotional styles? What could we do to reduce these limitations?

Buddha's Tears

These two images represent the passing of the Buddha from earthly life to Nirvana. Figure 3.1 is a hanging scroll from fourteenth-century Japan;

Figure 3.1 Death of the Historical Buddha (Nehan-zu), Hanging scroll; ink, colour, and gold on silk, Japan fourteenth century, The Metropolitan Museum of Art, New York

Figure 3.2 Par Nirvana, Qiao Bin, Earthenware with polychrome glaze, China 1503, The Metropolitan Museum of Art, New York

Figure 3.2 is a photograph of earthenware ceramics made by the artist Qiao Bin in 1503 for his private devotion. Both depictions are similar in surrounding the Buddha with attendants, who are weeping or have their mouths open. What purpose do the tears serve in these images? What do they represent? Do they tell us about emotion and whose? How would reflecting on art that represented people weeping shape devotional and spiritual practices?

Tears of Sorrow

The Passion of Christ, where through crucifixion Christ gave his life for the salvation of humanity, was strongly associated with both Christ and, his mother, Mary's sorrow in the medieval and early modern period. Christ's sorrow arose as he took on the sin and iniquity of humankind and had to account for them before God. Mary's sorrow came from watching her son die and through her motherly compassion towards humanity for their suffering. The Passion was understood as a sorrowful event and contemplating it was expected to produce sorrow in the

Figure 3.3 The Mourning Virgin; The Man of Sorrows, Posthumous Workshop Copy after Dieric Bouts, Oil on oak, Netherlandish, Leuven, ca. 1525, The Metropolitan Museum of Art, New York

Christian, making them aware of Christ's sacrifice, their own sin, and readying them for salvation. Figure 3.3 was a diptych – hinged wooden panels that could be closed like a book – and which were commonly used as altarpieces for worship. Figure 3.4 is a cheap black and white print of a painting of Mary of Sorrows that could have been purchased by ordinary people and displayed in their home. What message are the tears giving in these images? What emotion are they depicting? How would looking at these tears shape spiritual practice? Figures 3.1, 3.2, 3.3 and 3.4 come from different spiritual traditions. Are they doing similar work for their audiences, or something distinctive? What can this tell us about emotional cultures across the world?

Tears of Love

Figure 3.5 is a cheap print depicting a soldier leaving for war and his wife weeping beside him. Prints depicting departures between soldiers and their families, especially wives or girlfriends, were popular across the early modern period and well into the nineteenth century. What does his wife feel? How do we know this? What does the soldier feel? What can this tell us about marital relationships in seventeenth-century Germany?

Figure 3.4 Mater Dolorosa, Wallerant Vaillant, after Guido Reni, Dutch 1658–1677, Paper, h 231 mm × w 158 mm, Rijksmuseum, Amsterdam

Political Tears

During the eighteenth-century culture of sensibility, weeping was closely associated with moral sentiment. Both men and women of good character could evidence their pity, compassion or sorrow through displays of tears. However, weeping had to be considered authentic and sincere for it to be respected by onlookers. Excess tears could also cause problems, suggesting a lack of ability to apply self-control over the emotions. Figures 3.6 and 3.7 are satirical prints of the British politician Charles James Fox, leader of the Whig party, and known for his embrace of weeping as a manly mode. Figure 3.6 refers to a dispute in parliament in 1791 between Fox and Edmund Burke, previously his good friend, about the implications of the French Revolution for liberty, where Fox, when responding to Burke, burst into tears. It was an incident that resulted in

Figure 3.5 Afscheid van een soldaat, Julius Goltzius, Dutch 1560–1595, Paper engraving, w 276 mm × h 162 mm, Rijksmuseum, Amsterdam

Figure 3.6 Political Weeping Willow, British 1791, Paper etching 28.6 × 24.6 cm, Yale Center for British Art, Paul Mellon Collection

Figure 3.7 Tears of Sensibility – Sympathy a Poem – Let's all be Unhappy Together, Charles Ansell, British 1797, Paper etching 248 × 406 mm, Yale Center for British Art

numerous prints. Figure 3.7 shows a table full of 'Foxites', members of the Whig party especially associated with Fox's agenda, weeping after the arrest of Lord Edward Fitzgerald, Fox's first cousin, and leader of the United Irishmen. The latter had led an uprising in Ireland against the British State, inspired in part by revolutions in America and France. How should the reader interpret the tears in these images? What is their purpose? Are they associated with a particular emotion? Are they critical of weeping and how does the reader know this? What is the relationship between weeping and politics in these prints, and why might that be the case?

Legal Tears

Figure 3.8 features two Chinese prisoners in the pillory for some crime. The letters on the board explain the nature of the crime to the watching public. Figure 3.9 features a man in court being tried for a crime, while his sister cries beside him. The caption on the print reads 'The drunkard's children. plate V. from the bar of the gin-shop to the bar of the old bailey it is but one step', indicating it was one print in a moral tale. The prints are similar in featuring weeping women, looking upon crime. Why are they weeping? What message does their weeping give for the viewer of these prints? What can this tell us about weeping across culture?

Figure 3.8 Two Chinese prisoners with their necks enclosed in stocks known as the 'cangue', watched by a guard and a weeping woman. Gouache painting on rice-paper, 1780/1880?. Credit: Wellcome Collection, CC BY

Figure 3.9 'The Drunkard's Children'. A convicted thief stands on trial in a packed law court while his sister weeps. Coloured etching by G. Cruikshank, 1848, after himself. Credit: Wellcome Collection, CC BY

CONCLUSION

The prints above emerge from a wide range of time periods and cultural contexts, but they share some similarities. All of these tears are associated with emotions and events that we might consider 'negative'. Buddha's and Christ's death might play important spiritual functions for their faith – so ultimately be positive for humankind according to their beliefs – but they were marked by sorrow among their followers, an emotion expressed through tears but also facial gestures that suggest crying and distress, at least for a modern audience. The wife's tears at her soldier-husband are similarly suggestive of loss and distress, but not necessarily sorrow or grief. This representation shares with the religious iconography the idea that tears can also act as a mark of respect or a signal that the person who is absent is valued and important.

In contrast, the later set of prints are somewhat different. The tears of Fox and his followers, arising during a moment where weeping in public by men was culturally acceptable, nonetheless were used to ridicule their political position. Tears here became not only associated with Whiggish or democratic politics, but could be used to undermine manliness by suggesting they were excessive. If men were allowed to weep, they should exercise some control over their tears. The meaning of the legal tears is also somewhat different from the earlier prints. Both prints feature a woman weeping in response to a man's crime, but while the Chinese criminal also has tears, the British one does not. In neither print is the criminal going to die or be executed; their punishments are temporary. Therefore we may associate the weeping in these prints with the shame that the criminal's actions have brought on the family, and perhaps also associated hardships that come with losing a male breadwinner and their role in family life. The moral message of these prints is that criminal behaviour impacts not only on the individual, but the family.

It is interesting to contrast the tears that these criminal men produce in women with that of the departing soldier. Both prints consider how male behaviour produces female emotion, but in one instance the tears are a positive representation of love and marriage, and in the other an evidence of manly failure. Here the context of tears becomes central to their interpretation. It is also notable that all of these representations use tears to produce certain types behaviour in their viewers, whether that is to support religious devotion, to accept the necessity of men going to war (or alternatively to promote the importance of love in marriage), to shape public opinion on political issues, or to live an upstanding and moral life. Tears are not only used to represent emotion, but to direct the emotions and behaviours of others.

If these tears can begin a conversation about emotion in these historical periods, they are also suggestive of how we might read such sources for emotional styles. All of these prints are suggestive that weeping is appropriate in particular contexts within these cultures, although who is allowed to express emotion and how are somewhat varied. We might speculate that medieval Buddhists were permitted greater expression of sorrow as a bodily performance – given the focus on their movements and bodies as well as their tears – than early modern Europeans, where considerably more attention is given to the eyes and face as an evidence of grief. That early modern Europe might be more restrained in their presentation of sadness is also suggested by the print of the departing soldier, where tears are represented by a handkerchief and downward facial expression, rather than appearing themselves. In contrast, emotion in the later British prints appears more abundant. If the political tears are clearly ridiculous, even the crying woman in the courtroom seems to have abundant emotion, as the size and flowing shape of her handkerchief suggest. In contrast, the tears in the print of the Chinese prisoners are somewhat more restrained. If they are visible and accompany drooping faces, their bodies are more neutral and the woman's handkerchief smaller and more delicate.

From this, we might suggest something of the intensity of permitted emotional expression in these cultures, how bodies were deployed (or not) to express feeling, the uses of emotion in conveying information to viewers, and also how emotional expression was shaped by gender – some indications of an emotional style. From here we may wish to broaden out to other depictions of emotional expression to build a picture of whether such an exuberance was limited to the particular contexts found in these prints (death, the courtroom), or whether they marked a wider style of emotional behaviour for a group or entire society. Finally, we may wish to consider how individuals managed these emotional styles, through adapting them for their own use, in trying and failing to live up to emotional norms, or in finding an alternative emotional style, perhaps in a rare print that had wound its way across the world to a museum in the West.

FURTHER READING

Emotional Styles

*Gammerl, Benno. 'Emotional Styles – Concepts and Challenges.' *Rethinking History* 16, no. 2 (2012): 161–75.

Stearns, Peter. *American Cool: Constructing a Twentieth-Century Emotional Style*. New York: New York University Press, 1994.

*Stearns, Peter N., with Carol Z. Stearns. 'Emotionology: Clarifying the History of Emotions and Emotional Standards.' *The American Historical Review* 90, no. 4 (1985): 813–36.

Weeping

Begiato, Joanne. 'Tears and the Manly Sailor in England, c.1760–1860.' *Journal for Maritime Research* 17, no. 2 (2015): 117–33.

Broomhall, Susan. 'Facemaking: Emotional and Gendered Meanings in Chinese Clay Portraits of Danish Asiatic Company Men.' *Scandinavian Journal of History* 41, no. 3 (2016): 447–74.

Broomhall, Susan. 'Tears on Silk: Cross-Cultural Emotional Performances Among Japanese-Born Christians in Seventeenth-Century Batavia.' *Pakistan Journal of Historical Studies* 1, no. 1 (2016): 18–42.

Brown, Miranda. *The Politics of Mourning in Early China*. New York: SUNY Press, 2007.

Capp, Bernard. '"Jesus Wept" But Did the Englishman? Masculinity and Emotion in Early Modern England.' *Past and Present* 224, no. 1 (2014): 75–108.

Dixon, Thomas. 'Weeping in Space: Tears, Feelings, and Enthusiasm in Eighteenth-Century Britain.' In *Spaces for Feeling: Emotions and Sociabilities in Britain, 1650–1850*, ed. Susan Broomhall, 137–58. London: Routledge, 2015.

Dixon, Thomas. *Weeping Britannia: Portrait of A Nation in Tears*. Oxford: Oxford University Press, 2015.

Elkins, James. *Pictures & Tears: A History of People Who Have Cried in Front of Paintings*. London: Routledge, 2004.

Ellison, Julie. *Cato's Tears and the Making of Anglo-American Emotion*. Chicago: University of Chicago Press, 1999.

Gertsman, Elina, ed. *Crying in the Middle Ages*. London: Routledge, 2012.

Grey, Daniel. '"Agonised Weeping": Representing Femininity, Emotion and Infanticide in Edwardian Newspapers.' *Media History* 21, no. 4 (2015): 468–80.

Kutcher, Norman. *Mourning in Late Imperial China: Filial Piety and the State*. Cambridge: Cambridge University Press, 1999.

Liliequist, Jonas. 'The Political Rhetoric of Tears in Early Modern Sweden.' In *A History of Emotions, 1200–1800*, ed. Jonas Liliequist, 181–205. London: Pickering and Chatto, 2012.

Lutz, Tom. *Crying: The Natural and Cultural History of Tears*. New York: Norton, 1999.

Patton, Kimberley Christine, and John Stratton Hawley, eds. *Holy Tears: Weeping in the Religious Imagination*. Princeton and Oxford: Princeton University Press, 2005.

Sortkaer, Allan. 'The Little Girl Who Could Not Stop Crying: The Use of Emotions as a Signifier of True Conversion in Eighteenth-Century Greenland.' In *A History of Emotions, 1200–1800*, ed. Jonas Liliequist, 167–79. London: Pickering and Chatto, 2012.

Steggle, Matthew, *Laughing and Weeping in Early Modern Theatres*. London: Routledge, 2016.

Vaught, Jennifer C. *Masculinity and Emotion in Early Modern English Literature*. Hampshire: Ashgate, 2008.

4 Communities

If the term 'emotional community' had sometimes been used to capture the idea of social emotions in group contexts, the term was given its formal meaning for the field of the history of emotions by the historian Barbara Rosenwein. As a flexible concept that is easily applied to a range of examples, the concept of the emotional community has been one of the most popular ways of explaining how emotions are produced by particular groups and how they come to have a history. The downside of the popularity of the concept of emotional community is that sometimes the concept is applied a little too readily as a catchall term for exploring norms in emotional expression, without considering whether it is the most appropriate theory for the material at hand. This chapter introduces the idea of emotional communities and how it might be used by historians to aid their interpretation of their sources. It has a particular focus on popular literature produced in Peru and Argentina in the late nineteenth century, highlighting how a shared cultural norm around emotional expression and its relation to the moral self framed their understanding and practice of emotional life.

EMOTIONAL COMMUNITIES

An emotional community is not dissimilar from an emotional style, in that it seeks to understand group norms around the expression and evaluation of emotion. In a famous quote, Rosenwein described emotional communities as:

> precisely the same as social communities – families, neighbourhoods, parliaments, guilds, monasteries, parish church memberships – but the researcher looking at them seeks above all to uncover systems of feeling: what these communities (and the individuals within them) define and assess as valuable or harmful to them; the evaluations that they make about others' emotions; the nature of the affective bonds between people that they recognize; and the modes of emotional expression that they expect, encourage, tolerate, and deplore.[1]

As you can see, this is not dissimilar to the categories looked for when identifying an emotional style in that it incorporates ideas about emotion, how people express them, and how others judge and respond to those ideas. Like with an emotional style, an emotional community does not always have to be emotional, rather it is that they share the same attitudes, ideas and expressions about emotions that matter; some communities may be quite reserved in how they express emotion but still be an emotional community.

Emotional communities are different from styles in that there is a lot less emphasis on the 'gap' between a general style or norm for emotion and individual experience. Indeed, Rosenwein highlights that our concern about 'authentic' emotions, that we should prioritise as important what people feel *inside* over how they express that feeling, is quite specific to particular historic moments and cultures. Many societies would not make such a distinction between an internal and external self, or if they did, they may not necessarily prize the internal over the external as the most 'authentic'. Whilst Rosenwein acknowledges that there are contexts where people may wish or need to 'fake' emotion, she sees these as both rather specialist circumstances and as interesting in their own right for what they tell us about social expectations about emotion. Rather, in most instances, the expression of emotion can be considered to relate to personal experience and indeed, through language, to give shape and meaning to our feelings. Thus Rosenwein does not distinguish between emotion and affect, viewing them as describing the same thing.

For Rosenwein, a key advantage of the idea of emotional communities over that of style was that it allowed for considerable multiplicity within a single society. More recent work on styles that emphasises subcultures may downplay the significance of this difference between these concepts, but early work by Stearns and Stearns had focused on societal-level emotional cultures. Rosenwein suggested that, just as people live in a range of communities at once – from that of the village, to their workplace, to the household – each of which has its own emotion 'rules', so too could people live as part of a variety of emotional communities at once. As long as those communities were not remarkably different in their basic ideas and valuation of emotion, people generally could move quite easily across them. From this, she suggested that we could consider emotional communities as a series of overlapping circles, where a large societal-level emotional community would contain greater variety and more contest about emotional expression than smaller groups, whose norms would be narrower and more readily regulated by the group. If large groups contained variety in ideas about emotion, their differences should not be so significant that they did not share a core set of emotional practices and value system.

Emotional communities were initially closely attached to physical contexts or environments, so that they could readily be exchanged for places like a monastery or a town. This was partly as it was assumed that people raised in the same community would generally share the same understanding of emotion, as this was a required part of everyday communication. More recently, people have considered both what happens when someone 'strange' enters an emotional community – Rosenwein, for example, suggested that moving into a new physical space did not by itself make a stranger a part of the community – and also how communities can be built through textual and online communities, where shared values are more important than physical location. Rather than a focus on space, the capacity to meaningfully communicate emotion, interpret it and to share in valuing such expression became the defining features of a community.

Emotional communities have been criticised for being largely descriptive, rather than 'analytical', meaning that they can tell us what we see but not why it happens. This criticism emerges in part due to the fact that emotional communities were designed to respond to an influential claim by Norbert Elias that the history of emotion was a story of increasing self-control as people became more civilised. Medieval people, for Elias, were highly emotional, and so primitive, but later generations learned to manage their emotions as part of story of progress. Many historians disagreed with this sweeping claim, and the model of emotional communities was designed to show that, while some societies were more expressive than others, each community was similar in having rules to guide emotional experience. In having these rules, they were 'as civilised' as each other (or rather the idea of progress was not very helpful). One of the results of this is that a lot of work on emotional communities has been spent developing insight into how particular communities understood and expressed emotion, as part of a history that celebrates human variety and difference. There has been less work explicitly contrasting communities or considering what these differences mean for a more global understanding of the role of emotions in human life.

Some historians, of course, reject the need for such a universalising instinct, emphasising specificity and difference as a value in its own right. Moreover, emotional communities have been used, not least by Rosenwein, to help explain change over time in emotional expression, and broader power relationships. Rosenwein, particularly in her latest book *Generations of Feeling*, emphasised a model of change that was slow, incremental and that arose from the variety and multiplicity of communities within a society. Over time, some emotional values and expressions, responding to changing historical conditions or where new emotional ideas and experiences seem to work better for individuals and so become popularised, slowly evolved and were transformed. In this process, some emotions and emotional communities disappeared altogether; others were more tenacious. Rosenwein was especially interested in the concept of emotions as a form of 'inheritance' where the emotions of an older community could be retained or reformed by a later group, and even where an emotion that had fallen out of use could be redeployed by later generations on being rediscovered. Here she sought to offer some explanation for the continuation of some core ideas about emotion over very long historical periods, and even across communities over rather large spaces, like Europe. People's emotional worlds were similar not because emotions are universal, but because ideas about emotions can be widely circulated, influential and persistent in shaping experience.

Emotional communities can also help us explain power relationships in society, something that has been of less interest to Rosenwein than others who have picked up the concept in their work. Mark Seymour, for example, used the term 'emotional arena' to define moments within the emotional community where variation between groups came into conflict, and where certain values were given more normative power than others by the state.[2] One of the questions that arises here is whether lines of power in the emotional community really just reflect those within wider society and so those with structural power – judges in a courtroom, the monarch, landowners – ultimately decide emotional rules or whether the norms of the emotional community act as a constraint over the powerful. There is considerable evidence that emotional norms that are widely held can be used to constrain individual behaviour (and so power) at all social levels. Elite men who display an unmanly anger often face social condemnation in a similar way to those lower down the social ladder (although their power and wealth may help offset the consequences of such condemnation).

Individual resistance to or rejection of group norms is slightly different from when two different emotional cultures or values clash with each other, however, and in many respects mirrors clashes between the social groups who hold such values. Here Rosenwein's claim that emotional communities are 'precisely the same as social communities' comes to matter. Rather than considering emotional communities as a distinct form of social organisation, emotional communities are generally associated with pre-existing communities. A university can bring together people from very different cultural backgrounds and form them as a community, and as a community they might share certain norms around emotion, but an emotional community is generally accorded no such power of organisation. The idea that people might form a group with the explicit goal of expressing anger in a particular form and then build institutions that allow them to do that is not generally a feature of theories associated with the idea of an emotional community.[3] One result of this is that emotion is often located as a single strand within a history of a particular group, and so only plays one part in explanations for the operation of power, alongside more traditional explanations like money, political authority or gender.

A second result is that studies of emotional communities tend to consider other dimensions of communal experience as critical to understanding their emotions. Therefore, histories of emotional communities tend not only to explore how they evaluated and expressed emotion, but how their understanding of emotion operated in conjunction with other parts of society, perhaps religious practice, family relationships or the operation of the economy. Some historians of emotion find this focus on emotions as they operate in context distracting to the key purpose of the field (to chart a history of emotion); others argue that emotions do not exist in isolation from their uses and so require to be understood as embedded within wider social relationships and cultural practices. Emotional communities therefore tend to be a particularly important idea for those who prioritise emotional experience and practice in the everyday over providing definitions of emotion words or charting the frameworks of how emotions are understood.

APPLYING EMOTIONAL COMMUNITIES

As one of the most widely used concepts in the history of emotion, emotional communities have been deployed to interpret a wide range of types of source materials. Rosenwein's method for identifying an emotional community is similar to that described for identifying emotion words in Chap. 2. She suggested that historians should begin by gathering emotion words in documents that survive for the community under study and creating a 'bank' of terms as a starting point for analysis. Understanding the meaning of each word for that community is of course important to this analysis, but in developing a model of an emotional community, as significant is how those communities grouped words together.

Rosenwein suggests that, when people express emotion, they rarely use a single emotion word but rather express a range of words in particular contexts. We can see this is Chap. 2, where the writers of eighteenth-century love letters used not only the word 'love', but also 'affection', 'pleasure' and 'joy' in close correspondence. Exploring emotion words as clusters – those that appear regularly together – and as sequences, where one emotion is routinely followed by another, such as if the word 'anger' was routinely followed by 'sadness', can be used as the basis for understanding the logic of emotion for a particular community. Rosenwein also suggested that a model of an emotional community could be developed by identifying particular sites of emotion – her examples were heart, mind and spirit – and then interpreting the words associated with those sites as emotion words, allowing for a more flexible range of vocabulary to be incorporated into analysis of emotion than just words like 'anger' or 'love'.

As a focus on words like 'heart' and 'mind' suggests, Rosenwein was aware that emotions are indicated not just by language but our bodies, gestures and actions. Identifying and exploring these descriptions as part of emotional experience were also important to understanding the 'style' of an emotional community, but, as Rosenwein pointed out, very often how we accessed such descriptions of the body or behaviour was through descriptions in written texts, allowing a similar principle of exploring word clusters and sequences to be used here too. Scholars working with other sources, like paintings or films, have provided alternative ways of exploring emotional behaviour, that focus on analysing visual depictions. In a similar method to that used to develop word clusters, such analysis involves identifying repeated gestures, facial expressions or behaviours across sources, and looking at how they are deployed alongside other repeating imagery or social contexts.

Some historians, building on the idea that emotional communities are associated with particular social communities and that their emotions arise in situ, have been more interested in identifying emotional sites and then exploring how they operated. An example here might be recognising that religious devotion was considered to be an emotional practice – where devotional practices were designed to transform a person's feeling – and then to investigate not only how they described this change in feeling, but the rituals and environment used to enable this transformation. Exploring this may include not only personal narratives of emotional transformation but also descriptions of how the community conducted their devotional practices, such as through processions or church sermons. It may also include a study of ritual objects, their materiality and use, as part of the production of the emotional community. This method includes an attention to emotion words, but they are largely secondary to understanding the 'dynamics' of how emotions are produced through looking at the various props, bodily gestures and rituals that people use to enable an emotional transformation. For such historians, the emotional community consists of all of those who engage in such practices to enable emotional transformation – all who agree to follow this 'script' for emotional behaviour. Religious devotion, which sometimes can involve some unusual and rarely performed practices, might suggest that emotional communities can only be identified when doing something highly ritualised, but this model can be applied to most situations where people seek to manage, deploy or express emotion.

Popular literature, as appears in the examples below, can be one useful resource for developing a picture of an emotional community. Many types of popular literature are quite descriptive as the author tries to build a picture of the world they wish to convey. This means that we often have reasonably full descriptions of people, their emotions and the contexts in which they occurred. Popular literature is generally written for a large audience, and while sometimes an author might 'miss the mark', we can assume that the content would be explicable to many people in the society in which they were produced. By this I mean that it is likely that most readers could identify with the emotional behaviours and experiences described and consider them to bear some relation to their own lives or those of people around them. In this, we might say that the author did a good job at 'capturing' the norms of the emotional community of which they were a part.

Sometimes authors describe people who are unusual or extraordinary. When this happens, an author might signal this to the reader in various ways – by noting the fact – or having characters respond with surprise or misbelief. But sometimes a historian might not realise this is happening. This is where reading widely and developing a broader understanding of the culture can be useful for helping us identify when behaviour is meant to be considered 'strange' or when it is part of ordinary experience for that community. As in the examples below, sometimes even extraordinary behaviour can be explained within a community's emotional framework, such as when somebody who had a mental illness is portrayed as overly affectionate or violent. Their behaviour may be considered inappropriate, but it can still be explained by the cultural logic of how emotion works and the factors that influence that. Historians of emotion using popular sources are not necessarily looking for 'real-life' examples of people's emotions, but rather seek to understand how the emotional community that produced such literature understood and valued emotions within the contexts described. It may also tell us something of the role of literature within a particular community. Literature can have particular emotional functions for some groups, such as developing empathy in the reader or acting to educate readers in appropriate emotional responses to particular situations. Here we can also consider how the literature we are reading plays a role in the rituals of the emotional community, as well as describing their beliefs or values.

EMBODIED EMOTIONS

The writing below was produced in the second half of the nineteenth century in South America. While both pieces are considered important pieces of South American literature, they incorporate some popular ideas about emotion that were widely held across the globe. This is not surprising given that both authors were well educated and so widely read in world literatures, and part of communities that had been colonised by Europeans, so had close cultural ties with that part of the world. Both literatures rely on the science of 'physiognomy', which was a belief system that thought the body could be interpreted for evidence of moral character. Physiognomy, sometimes called phrenology, paid special attention the face and head, in terms of both its shape and make up (e.g. was there a large forehead and dark brows, or narrow cheekbones?), and the expressions people made with their faces.

The science of physiognomy, promoted in the nineteenth century by Johann Kaspar Lavater, taught people that by careful attention to physical features and emotional expression a person's personality and character could be ascertained. For the experts in the field, this was expected to be a subtle art. Someone might have eyebrows that indicated a certain weakness of character, but a strong jaw, indicating manly firmness. Rather than faces and bodies providing straightforward messages to the viewer, different parts were combined together to provide a complex indicator of the inner person. The challenges with doing this meant that it was an 'art' that was also subject to considerable ridicule in the popular press as people attempted to do this themselves and made fun of others who did so. Yet, that it was subject to such mockery was indicative of how widespread knowledge of this 'science' was. Moreover, even if people thought that the art of reading people's faces accurately was unlikely to lead to an exact measure of character, the larger principle that people's bodies, and especially beauty, was related to moral character was a very old cultural idea dating to the medieval period and found in a wide range of European literature. Lavater applied scientific principles to a longstanding association between beauty and goodness, ugliness and sin.

This close association between the physical body and moral character meant that physical descriptions of people's body, and especially their faces, were not just used to describe what someone looked like but also to tell a story about their character. As a result, many writings of the nineteenth century spend considerable time on such accounts and use them to set the emotional 'tone' of a piece of writing. A character whose physical features are suggestive of aggression or anger would be understood by readers as a potential 'bad guy', one who was beautiful and calm, suggestive of their moral goodness. The reader might feel some ominous dread when reading about a man with heavy eyebrows and an overbearing brow, and invest in the beautiful female character. Descriptions of emotion by characters too could have narrative functions. Expressions of sorrow might indicate the victim of the story, while anger – depending on whether it was just or not – might help locate the person's role in the story plot.

If some features of this writing are distinctive to a global scientific model for moral emotions, others are indicative of South American cultural ideals (not always dissimilar from their Spanish ancestors). The importance of a Christian patriarchal social order, where subordinates should respect their godly elders but where in turn those elders should exercise their moral responsibilities to their subordinates, was a central idea. Within this society, boys – being prepared for their role as patriarchs – were expected to exercise self-control over their emotions and to behave with appropriate respect for those placed above them. Women in comparison were provided space for a greater level of emotional expression. The influence of the educational philosopher Jean-Jacques Rousseau and his many followers is also suggested in the ways that character, and its relation to emotional expression, is viewed as a product of environment and social conditions; and ideas from the Scottish Enlightenment are suggested in the paralleling of emotional self-control with level of 'civilisation'. Thus, a society that produces uncontrollable emotion is less advanced than others. These ideas underpinned the interpretation of bodies and emotions in these texts, providing a critical context for the reader's interpretation of the material before them. The bodies and emotions described in these books were interpreted by readers through these cultural lenses, and that informed how they evaluated what was going on.

Being able to interpret the meanings of physical descriptions of the body as moral character, or to understand emotion as indicative of the roles of characters in a story plot, required readers to share a common understanding of bodies, emotions, their relation to moral character, and how all three were produced. This required them to share the same valuation of particular emotional expressions as good or bad. Understanding bodies and emotions in this way, and ideally responding yourself with appropriate emotions, whether of anticipation, excitement, dread or so forth in relation to the story, required being part of a shared emotional community. Thus the historian who can come to understand the 'emotion work' these texts are doing for their reader can begin to access the emotional world of their historical subjects. Interestingly in this case, the emotional community being drawn on requires both some local knowledge about South American culture, and especially colonialism, and also a 'scientific' model for understanding bodies that was influential across the globe at the historical moment these authors were writing.

INTERPRETING EMOTIONS ON THE BODY

Popular writing – from novels to non-fiction – provides insight into emotional communities through providing access to well-known ideas, values and beliefs about emotion, their expected uses and meanings. Below are excerpts from two nineteenth-century nationalist South American writers. The first is a work of creative non-fiction by Domingo Sarmiento, exploring the history and culture of Argentina, and especially the rise to power of Facundo Quiroga, a 'gaucho' or skilled horseman, who became Governor of La Rioja and a leader of federalism in the 1830s and 1840s. Sarmiento was a political activist, writer and journalist who eventually became president of Argentina. The second excerpt is from Clorinda Matto de Turner's novel, *Birds Without a Nest*, an early example of 'indigenismo', literature designed to draw attention to the experience of indigenous people in colonial South America. Matto de Turner was a Peruvian journalist of Spanish descent and campaigner for indigenous rights. She translated the gospels into Quechua. *Birds Without a Nest* was highly controversial both due to its unflattering portrayal of the church and as it showed a romantic relationship between a White man and an indigenous woman. Her writing led to her ex-communication by the church, and eventually she fled to exile in Argentina. Both of the works below are excerpted from nineteenth- and early-twentieth-century translations into English.

Begin by reading through the texts, and then summarise what they are both about. Is there an evident storyplot or message? What characters are found in each piece of writing? What role do they play in it? Are there other 'active' elements that are shaping the narrative (the nation, landscape, material goods)? Are they the same kind of writing, or do they have differences in genre or style? Are there things that both pieces of writing have in common? Or anything that is significantly different from each other? Why do you think the author was writing? Who was their intended audience? How might the information we have on the author shape our interpretation of the text? What would happen if we knew nothing about them? Would it make a difference? How do you think translation might affect the meanings of these texts?

From this, we might explore how these texts help us to develop an understanding of the nature of the emotional community the authors are writing for. Can we identify any emotion words or clusters? Are there any sequences of emotions evident here? Other than words, are there any 'props' or 'tools' that we can identify as being important in how this community produce emotion? How are emotions expressed in this community? What role is the body playing in these texts? What messages is the author giving about the characters through their descriptions of bodies and their expressions and behaviours? What emotions do they value or disdain? How do we know that? How does the emotional expression described here relate to emotion words, bodily gesture, or other dimensions of emotional life?

Reading these two texts together, how does Sarmiento's text help us better interpret Matto de Turner, and vice versa? Are there clues in one text about emotion that help us better understand what is happening in the other? Can we start to build a picture of emotional rules for this community? What are these rules? How do we know this? What role does emotion play in producing morality for these writers? What does this tell us about how they understand emotion to operate? Can this be the basis of an emotional community? Who is the 'emotional community' that we are studying through these examples? Do we need to understand more about the audience? How might the translation of these texts into English affect our understanding of the emotional community? Does using a translation change who the emotional community we are studying is?

1. Domingo F. Sarmiento, *Life in the Argentine Republic in the Days of the Tyrants; or Civilization and Barbarism*, ed. Mrs. [Mary Tyler Peabody] Horace Mann (New York: Hurd and Houghton, 1868), 32–41, 76–89.

The most conspicuous and extraordinary of the occupations to be described, is that of the Rastreador, or track-finder. All the gauchos of the interior are Rastreadores. In such extensive plains, where paths and lines of travel cross each other in all directions, and where the pastures in which the herds feed are unfenced, it is necessary often to follow the tracks of an animal, and to distinguish them among a thousand others, and to know whether it was going at an easy or rapid pace, at liberty or led, laden or carrying no weight. ... The Rastreador proper is a grave, circumspect personage, whose declarations are considered conclusive evidence in the inferior courts. Consciousness of the knowledge he possesses, gives him a certain reserved and mysterious dignity. Every one treats him with respect; the poor man because he fears to offend one who might injure him by a slander or an accusation; and the proprietor because of the possible value of his testimony. ...

The Baqueano is a grave and reserved gaucho, who knows every span of twenty thousand square leagues of plain wood, and mountain! He is the most thorough topographer, the only map which a general consults in directing the movements of his campaign. The Baqueano is always at his side. Modest and mute as a garden-wall, he is in possession of every secret of the campaign; the fate of the army, the issue of a battle, the conquest of a province, all depend upon him. The Baqueano almost always discharges his duty with fidelity, but the general does not place full confidence in him. ...

The Gaucho Outlaw. The example of this type of character, to be found in certain places, is an outlaw, a squatter, a kind of misanthrope. He is Cooper's Hawkeye or Trapper, with all the knowledge of the wilderness possessed by the latter; and with all the aversion to the settlements of the whites, but without his natural morality or his friendly relations with the savages. The name of gaucho outlaw is not applied to him wholly as an uncomplimentary epithet. The law has been for many years in pursuit of him. His name is dreaded – spoken under the breath, but not in hate, and almost respectfully. He is a mysterious personage; his abode is the pampa; his lodgings are the thistle fields; he lives on partridges and hedgehogs ... This white-skinned savage, at war with society and proscribed by the laws, is no more depraved at heart than the inhabitants of the settlements. The reckless outlaw who attacks a whole troop, does no harm to the traveller. The gaucho outlaw is no bandit, or highwayman ... To be sure, he steals; but this is his profession, his trade, his science. ...

There are, in fact, as is proved by phrenology and comparative anatomy, relations between external forms and moral qualities, between the countenance of man and that of some animal whose disposition resembles his own. Facundo, as he was long called in the interior, – or, General Don Facundo Quiroga, as he afterwards became, when society had received him into its bosom and victory had crowned him with laurels – was a stoutly built man of low stature, whose short neck and broad shoulders supported a well-shaped head, covered with a profusion of black and closely curling hair. His somewhat oval face was half buried in this mass of hair and an equally thick black, curly beard, rising to his cheek-bones, which by their prominence evidenced a firm and tenacious will. His black and fiery eyes, shadowed by thick eyebrows, occasioned an involuntary sense of terror in those on whom they chanced to fall, for Facundo's glance was never direct, whether from habit or intention. With the design of making himself always formidable, he always kept his head bent down, to look at one from under his eyebrows, like the Ali Pacha of Monovoisin. The image of Quiroga is recalled to me by the Cain represented by the famous Ravel troupe, setting aside the artistic and statuesque attitudes, which do not correspond to his. To conclude, his features were regular and the pale olive of his complexion harmonized well with the dense shadows which surrounded it.

... Quiroga possessed those natural qualities which converted the student of Brienne into the Genius of France ... Such natures develop according to the society in which they originate and are either noble leaders who hold the high-est place in history, ever forwarding the progress of civilization or the cruel and vicious tyrants who become the scourges of their race and time. ... In the house in which he lodged [as a youth], he could never be induced to take his seat at the family table; in school he was haughty, reserved and unsocial; he never joined the other boys except to head their rebellious proceedings or to beat them. The master, tired of contending with so untameable a disposition, on one occasion provided himself with a new and stiff strap, and said to the frightened boys, as he showed it to them, "This is to be made supple upon Facundo." Facundo, then eleven years old, heard this threat, and the next day he tested its value. Without having learned his lesson, he asked the head-master to hear it himself, because, as he said, the assistant was unfriendly to him. The master complied with the request. Facundo made one mistake, then two, three, and four; upon which the master used his strap upon him. Facundo, who had calculated everything, down to the weakness of the chair in which the master was seated, gave him a buffet, upset him on his back, and, taking to the street in the confusion created by this scene, hid himself among some wild vines where they could not get him out for three days. Was not such a boy the embryo chieftain who would afterwards defy society at large?

In early manhood his character took a more decided cast, constantly becom-ing more gloomy, imperious, and wild. From the age of fifteen years he was irresistibly controlled by the passion for gambling, as is often the case with such natures, which need strong excitement to awaken their dormant energies. This made him notorious in the city, and intolerable in the house which afforded him its hospitality; and finally under this influence, by a shot fired at one George Peña, he shed the first rill of blood which went to make up the wide torrent that marked his way through life. ... When he was addressed as General, and had colonels at his orders, he had two hundred lashes given of them in his house at San Juan, for having, as he said, cheated at play. He ordered two hundred lashes to be given to a young man for having allowed himself a jest at a time when jests were not to his taste; and two hundred lashes was the penalty afflicted on a woman in Mendoza for having said to him as he passed, "Farewell, General," when he was going off in a rage at not having succeeded in intimidating a neigh-bour of his, who was a peaceable and judicious as Facundo was rash and gaucho-like.

And here ends the private life of Quiroga, in which I have omitted a long series of deeds which only show his evil nature, his bad education and his fierce and bloody instincts. The facts stated appear to me to sum up the whole public life of Quiroga. I see in them the great man, the man of genius, in spite of him-self and unknown to himself a Caesar, Tamerlane, or Mohammed. The fault is not his that thus he was born. ... With these remarks is connected by imperceptible links the motto of this chapter, "He is the natural man, as yet unused either to repress or disguise his passions; he does not restrain their energy, but gives free rein to their impetuosity. This is the character of the human race."

2. Clorina Matto de Turner. *Birds Without a Nest: A Story of Indian Life and Priestly Oppression in Peru*, trans. J.G.H. (London: Charles J. Thynne, 1904), 13–26.

... a labourer crossed the plaza, guiding his yoke of oxen laden with the implements of husbandry, a yoke, a grad and leathern straps for work, and the provisions of the day; the traditional "chuspa," or bag of woven wool of various colours, fastened to the belt containing the "coca" leaves and cakes of "llipta" for his lunch.

On passing the door of the temple he reverently lifted his cap and murmured something like an invocation, then went on his way, now and then looking back sorrowfully at the cabin from whence he came.

Was it fear or doubt, love or hope that troubled his soul at that moment? It was plainly to be seen that something impressed his mind strongly.

Scarcely was the labourer lost to sight in the distance when the figure of a woman sprang lightly over the wall on the South side of the plaza. She was a young Indian woman of not more than thirty years of age, with fine features and a rosy face. Shaking off her dress the mud which had fallen upon her from the wall, she directed her steps to a modest looking white cottage with tiled roof not far away.

At the open door she was met by a young lady neatly dressed in grey with lace trimmings and mother-of-pearl buttons.

Very fair and generous was this lady, – the Señora Lucia, wife of Don Fernando Marin, a gentleman who had some business connection with the mines near the place and had settled temporarily in Killac.

The newcomer addressed Lucia quickly without ceremony, saying: "In the name of the Virgin, Señora, protect this day an unfortunate family. He who has gone to the fields to-day passing by you here, laden with the implements of labour, is Juan Yupanqui, my husband and father of our two little girls. Alas, Señora! He has gone out with his heart half dead, because he knows that to-day will be the day of distribution, and as the overseer directs the barley sowing he cannot hide himself because, beside the imprisonment, he would have to pay the fine, and we have no money. I was crying beside Rosalia, who sleeps by the fireplace, when suddenly my heart told me that you are good, and without Juan's knowledge I came to implore your assistance for the sake of the Virgin, Señora.

A flood of tears put an end to that supplication which was full of mystery to Lucia, for, having resided but a few months in the place, she was ignorant of its customs and could not appreciate at their full value the references made by the poor woman, although they roused her sympathy.

It is necessary to see face to face these disinherited creatures, to hear from their own lips in their expressive language the narrative of their actual circumstances, in order to understand the quick sympathy which springs up unconsciously in noble hearts, and how they came to take part in their suffering finally, although at first prompted only by a desire for knowledge. ...

Lucia was no ordinary woman. She had received a good education, and by means of comparisons, her quick intelligence often reached the light of truth in advance of others. She was tall and graceful, not very fair, but what is called in the country "pearl coloured"; her beautiful eyes were shaded by long lashes and velvety eyebrows; she had also that distinctively feminine charm, a wealth of long wavy hair. She had not quite completed twenty summers, but marriage had set upon her that sign and seal of lady that so well becomes a young woman who understands how to unite amiability of character with seriousness of manner. ... The first thought that came to her was to speak personally with the priest and the Governor. ...

Of low stature, flat head, large wide-open nose, thick lips, small grey eyes; a short neck surrounded by a band of black and white beads, unshaven chin, dressed in a habit of black cloth, badly cut and badly attended to, a hat of Guyaquil straw in his right hand, – such was the aspect of the first personage who entered, whom Lucia saluted with much respect, saying, "May God be with you, Father Pascual."

The priest, Pascual Vargas, successor of Don Pedro Miranda y Claro, in the holy office at Killac, inspired from the first very serious doubts as to the idea of his having learned in the Seminary either Theology or Latin. His age bordered on fifty years. His manner and appearance were such that it was not difficult to understand Marcela's reluctance to enter the parochial house in the character of a "mita." ...

The personage enveloped in a large Spanish cloak, who followed the priest into the room, was Don Sebastian Pancorbo, Governor of the town of Killac.

Don Sebastian, after passing three years in a primary school in a neighbouring city, returned to his native town, married Doña Petronilla Hinojosa, daughter of one of the notables of the place, and was immediately made Governor; that is to say, he arrived at the highest post known and aspired to in a small town.

These two grand personages seated themselves comfortably in the arm chairs indicated by Lucia.

The Señora Marin set herself to the task of interesting her callers in the favour of Marcela. Addressing herself particularly to the priest, she said: "In the name of the Christian religion, which is pure love, tenderness and hope; in the name of your Master, who commanded us to give to the poor, – I ask you, Father, to pardon this debt which weighs upon the family of Juan Yupanqui. Ah! You will have in exchange double treasure in heaven!"

"Señora," replied the priest, settling himself comfortably and resting both hands upon the arms of the chair, "all these are beautiful theories, but God help us who live without income? To-day, with the increase of ecclesiastical taxes, and the rush of civilised people who will come with the railroads, our emoluments will cease, and ... and ... in short Doña Lucia, away with the priests! We will die with hunger!"

"Has the Indian Yupanqui come for this?" interposed the Governor in support of the priest, and with a triumphant tone concluded, emphasising the words for Lucia's benefit: "You know, Señora, that custom is law, and that no one can take us out of our customs."

"Gentlemen, charity is also a law of the heart," interrupted Lucia.

"And Juan, eh? We will see if he will return to touch these springs again, this mischief-making Indian," continued Pancorbo in a threatening tone, that could not help being noticed by Lucia, whose heart trembled with fear.

The few words exchanged between them made perfectly clear to Lucia the moral degradation of these men, from whom nothing could be hoped and everything was to be feared.

CONCLUSION

Both of these texts place considerable emphasis on the body as a symbol of moral character, describing at length how a person looked and tying it to their behaviours, actions and emotions. Sarmiento introduces the reader to a variety of types of gaucho, where looks, personality, occupation and behaviour each reinforced the other. The Baqueano is defined not just by his job, but by the internal characteristics that led him to choose this job. Yet, as Sarmiento suggests in his text, the job too shapes the man; people are products of both nature and environment together. Emotion is identified as significant here both because character shapes how people express emotion – whether they are kind and sympathetic, or passionate and angry – and because people should respond emotionally to different types of character (we respond with trust, low confidence or dread). Sarmiento explicitly explains the 'logic' of character, drawing on phrenology, in his writing.

Matte de Turner does not explicitly acknowledge the underpinning science beneath her narrative, but her lengthy descriptions of the body and the ways that we are expected to read those descriptions as a proxy for personal character are suggestive that they both share a common understanding of the body. Sarmiento's more explicit discussion of the 'logic' of his analysis can then be used to help us interpret Matte de Turner's text. *Birds Without a Nest* uses many more emotion words that Sarmiento ('fear', 'doubt', 'love', 'hope', 'sympathy'); her characters show more emotion on their bodies and express feeling explicitly with words. This appears designed to promote sympathy in the reader and to highlight the emotional sophistication of a group – the indigenous Peruvians – who were sometimes associated with 'primitive' feeling and so thought to be less civilised. It may also reflect gendered norms around expressing emotion, as her characters are mainly female, compared with Sarmiento's focus on men. Sarmiento uses less direct emotion words, but replaces them with others that have a similar impact on the reader – 'hospitality', 'confusion', 'blood'. These are ideas that are closely associated with emotion and emotional events. Hospitality was an 'emotion-laden' concept, an evidence of Christian charity (so love) and which was built on trust, care and kindness. Breaching hospitality was not only rude, but violated some important social values, making Facundo's behaviour more horrifying for readers.

Reading these texts together, the historian can start to build a picture of the 'emotional community' of the author and readership for these texts. Emotion for this group was largely viewed as a biological function, rather than an operation of the soul or spirit, and so tied to the body. But, drawing on a long Christian heritage where passion led people to sin, emotion was still strongly associated with moral action. This meant that some emotions – love, hope, but perhaps even doubt and sorrow – could be valued positively due to their association with moral behaviour, and others like rage, greed and even 'passion' (as an excessive emotion) could be valued negatively. Emotions are also represented as contagious, through sympathy, so that one person's sorrow could move a moral person to pity and to take action; displays of rage could evoke dread or fear. This extended not only to emotional exchanges in person but through writing and descriptions on the page. We might suggest that the emotional 'style' of this community is quite expressive in general (even if some outbursts are disapproved of), but where women were allowed more space to display and express emotion than men, who were encouraged to be reserved and exercise self-control.

Moving forward, we may wish to read a wider range of texts to see how typical these examples are, and whether there is any variety within this community. To best understand this culture, we should also read some texts in Spanish to consider how translation might shape the emotional community depicted here. Literary texts are helpful in evidencing cultural beliefs, but both of the texts above have 'moral' and 'political' purposes, trying to persuade the public to recognise the injustice they identify. It may be that the use of emotion here is somewhat different to other contexts. Comparing these texts with different genres of writing, or non-written sources, might help build a more complex analysis of the emotional community identified here.

FURTHER READING

Emotional Communities

Broomall, James. '"We Are a Band of Brothers": Manhood and Community in Confederate Camps and Beyond.' *Civil War History* 60, no. 3 (2014): 270–309.

Broomhall, Susan, and Jacqueline Van Gent. 'Corresponding Affections: Emotional Exchange Among Siblings in the Nassau Family.' *Journal of Family History* 34, no. 2 (2009): 143–65.

Lynch, Andrew. 'Emotional Community.' In *Early Modern Emotions: An Introduction*, ed. Susan Broomhall, 3–6. London and New York: Routledge, 2017.

Plamper, Jan. 'The History of Emotions: An Interview with William Reddy, Barbara Rosenwein, and Peter Stearns.' *History and Theory* 49, no. 2 (2010): 237–65.

Rosenwein, Barbara. 'Worrying About Emotions in History.' *American Historical Review* 107, no. 3 (2002): 821–45.

Rosenwein, Barbara. *Emotional Communities in the Early Middle Ages*. New York: Cornell University Press, 2006.

*Rosenwein, Barbara. 'Problems and Methods in the History of Emotions.' *Passions in Context* 1 (2010). www.passionsincontext.de/uploads/media/01_Rosenwein.pdf

*Rosenwein, Barbara. *Generations of Feeling: A History of Emotions, 600–1700*, 1–15. Cambridge: Cambridge University Press, 2015.

Physiognomy

Barclay, Katie. 'Performing Emotion and Reading the Male Body in the Irish Court, c.1800–1845.' *Journal of Social History* 51, no. 2 (2017): 293–312.

Hartley, Lucy. *Physiognomy and the Meaning of Expression in Nineteenth-Century Culture*. Cambridge: Cambridge University Press, 2008.

Parssinen, T. M. 'Popular Science and Society: The Phrenology Movement in Early Victorian Britain.' *Journal of Social History* 8 (1974): 1–20.

South American Emotions

Graham, Heather, and Lauren G. Kilroy-Ewbank. *Visualizing Sensuous Suffering and Affective Pain in Early Modern Europe and the Spanish Americas*. Leiden: Brill, 2018.

Holler, Jacqueline. 'Flight and Confinement Female Youth, Agency, and Emotions in Sixteenth-Century New Spain.' In *The Youth of Early Modern Women*, eds. Elizabeth Storr Cohen and Margaret Louise Reeves, 97–116. Amsterdam: Amsterdam University Press, 2018.

Lipsett-Rivera, Sonya. 'The Power of Laughter: Humor, Violence and Consensus in New Spain. 17th and 18th Centuries.' *Revista de Historia Social y de las Mentalidades* 19, no. 2 (2015): 239–63.

Lipsett-Rivera, Sonya. 'The Emotional Life of Boys in Eighteenth-Century Mexico City.' In *The Routledge History Handbook of Gender and the Urban Experience*, eds. Deborah Simonton et al., 351–62. London: Routledge, 2017.

Seed, Patricia. *To Love, Honour and Obey in Colonial Mexico: Conflicts over Marriage Choice, 1574–1821*. Stanford: Stanford University Press, 1988.

Seed, Patricia. 'Narratives of Don Juan: The Language of Seduction in Seventeenth-Century Hispanic Literature and Society.' *Journal of Social History* 26, no. 4 (1993): 745–68.

Villa-Flores, Javier, and Sonya Lipsett-Rivera, eds. *Emotions and Daily Life in Colonial Mexico*. Albuquerque: University of New Mexico Press, 2014.

5 Regimes

An emotional regime is an idea developed by the historian and anthropologist William Reddy to explain how norms for emotional lives can operate as a form of power that restricts human behaviour and affirms the authority of powerful groups. Reddy was particularly interested in the question of whether we could still make a case for 'natural human rights' in a post-modern world, which was considered to promote 'relativism', the idea that there is no universal truth but that each culture has its own – equally valid – moral system. If all systems were equally valid, what basis do humans have to claim that some systems are immoral or cruel, we might ask? Rosenwein promotes a less extreme form of relativism in her model of emotional communities that emphasises that communities have infinite variety but are not more or less civilised than each other. Reddy felt that it was still important in the modern world to be able to condemn actions that caused suffering and to promote models of social life that enabled human flourishing. Emotional regimes offered him a way to explain the possibility of human suffering, despite the fact that emotions are deeply shaped by cultural rules and are thus a learned behaviour. This chapter explores the nature of an emotional regime, the importance of 'emotives' to this concept, and how to apply these ideas to historical sources. It has a particular focus on slavery in nineteenth-century North America and the narratives produced by slaves about their experiences of living in this emotional regime.

EMOTIONAL REGIMES

If Stearns and Stearns' 'styles' posited a meaningful gap between language and the body, and Rosenwein's 'community' did not differentiate between language and physical experience, Reddy sought a compromise between these positions. Reddy believes that there is a physical materiality beyond language – that bodily feeling does not require language – but that language is not simply 'representational' – it is not just a label that we attach to experience. Rather Reddy emphasises the way that language gives shape to experience, but that it can never quite fully capture feeling.

To describe this, Reddy draws on 'speech act theory', which argues that when we speak we do not just describe things but 'do' things. When somebody says 'I do' during the wedding ceremony, they create a binding legal contract – their words were 'active' in changing a person's marital status. In a similar way, when we use words to name what we are feeling, we do not just describe that feeling but give it shape and function. Reddy describes the emotion label that we place on our feeling (e.g. anger) as an 'emotive'. An emotive is a special category of word that does not just describe, but produces feeling. When we label our feeling as anger, we attach to that feeling all the ideas, experiences and actions that we associate with that term (just as naming an animal 'tiger' brings with it certain associations and actions), and this in turn shapes how we respond to that feeling (whether we punch someone or leave the room). Naming our emotions also has an impact on our feelings, because when we label our feeling anger we may then have to adjust our feelings accordingly to match up more precisely with the cultural ideal, perhaps by increasing the intensity of our emotion to enable us to punch someone.

Reddy describes this process of figuring out our feeling, naming it, then adjusting our feelings to better correspond to the label, as a process of 'navigation'. Here the experience of emotion is a striving to make sense of our inner world by helping it line up with ideas from our culture. Erin Sullivan calls this process, which for her includes our bodily gestures and expressions as well as words, 'emotional improvisation', emphasising that the experience of emotion is just not limited to finding the right label, but also adjusting our emotions to our bodies and surrounding environment.[1] Thus, we may label our emotion 'anger' and so, according to cultural scripts around anger, know that we should punch the person who made us angry. But while that might be acceptable with a social equal, or in a place like a pub, we might recognise that we should not punch a child or punch anyone in church. Thus, if an emotive provides a certain framing for our feeling, how we manage that emotion might not be identical in every environment, but require a process of exploration of both feeling and the appropriate way to manifest it. Importantly, if this model suggests a gap between felt experiences and language, both the body and culture act together to produce emotion, both sides of the divide shaping each other.

Unfortunately for humans, the process of naming feeling is often unsatisfactory. At a basic level, this is because words can never perfectly capture what they describe, especially when we are discussing something as complex and abstract as a feeling. But in some instances, our sense of dissatisfaction is more significant than at others. Sometimes the language we have to describe our feelings feels inadequate to the task, or the script associated with a particular emotion may seem inappropriate. Punching someone may be the expected response to anger, but we find that this hurts our hand and so wish to avoid punching people. Here our experience of pain challenges normative expectations of how to 'do' anger, and so we become unhappy with the normal codes for expressing anger. Reddy describes this experience of becoming unhappy with norms for emotion as 'emotional suffering', and he explains it through a concept called the 'emotional regime'.

An emotional regime is a set of widespread values for emotion that people are expected to conform to. Reddy defines it as 'the set of normative emotions and the official rituals, practices, and emotives that express and inculcate them; a necessary underpinning of any stable political regime'.[2] In many ways, this is similar to the rules for emotional expression that are found within the concept of an emotional style or emotional community. However, Reddy goes further in emphasising their importance to the operation of power, where the normative rules for expressing and responding to emotion become part of political life. Conforming your own emotions to that norm can become a significant expectation by the state or other institution (like a church or even the family), whereby if you do not emote appropriately for a particular context then you may be punished. Not expressing your love of nation in a highly patriotic regime may lead to your arrest for treason; refusing to feel sorrow at the death of your father may lead to your expulsion from your family. As a result, many people will make an attempt to conform their emotions to the expected norm so as not to risk political expulsion or punishment. For many people – those whose personal experiences and feelings conform well to the emotional regime – this is not hard to do. Indeed, lots of groups experience this process of aligning personal feeling with cultural norms as a smooth, naturalised process (they do not need to think about it too much). However not everyone finds this easy.

When people cannot conform their emotions to the norm – that is, when they experience emotional suffering – they may look for opportunities to express their preferred feelings, often gathering like-feeling people around them. Reddy describes these opportunities as 'emotional refuges', places where people can express their emotions freely without risk of punishment. Emotional refuges are not without emotional rules, but rather develop their own norms and cultures for emotional expression that align more closely with the experience of their members. A number of scholars have used this idea to explain the importance of homosexual subcultures and spaces for allowing gay men and women space to express their feelings, especially in cultures where such feeling was illegal or disliked. Emotional refuges are important when explaining 'regime changes' within an emotional regime. Over time, an emotional refuge might expand and become more politically important until their emotional rules become the dominant norm for emotional life.

For Reddy, who tied emotional regimes to political regimes, a change in an emotional regime would be accompanied by a change in political regime. But in other contexts, the transformation may not require the removal of an institution but rather an over-arching change of culture, which may include the same actors. For example, a family that went to relationship counselling may learn that trying to control how individuals felt about death was harmful to the survival of the institution, and so adapt their emotional regime to address this problem and become more inclusive. Here the people involved did not change, but – inspired perhaps by emotional suffering amongst their members – they adapted their emotional culture. Reddy argues that there are more or less liberal emotional regimes, so some institutions (nations, families) allow more opportunity for people not to conform to the emotional rules than others, or allow more space for emotional variety. He believes that the goal for a political regime should be 'emotional liberty', where people have a greater degree of emotional freedom so as to minimise emotional suffering.

Emotional liberty is one of Reddy's most controversial concepts as he does not believe this is a 'relative value', that is a value that might be adjusted across culture, but an absolute idea. He believes this is necessary for his theory to contribute to broader political claims for human rights, one of which should be a right to emotional liberty. Emotional liberty is a concept that we should be able to apply to any period and use to judge other societies as 'good' or 'bad' (or rather, more or less liberal). Other historians suggest that emotional liberty could be used without being absolute, so that we could judge past societies by the amount of emotional suffering experienced by their own communities, rather than by comparing their society with a universal standard. A regime that highly controlled the emotions of its members but where people were happy with this and experienced little suffering might be considered 'good', rather than 'bad'.

Another part of his theory that has been contested by later users of the term is his insistence on the 'unconscious' as part of emotional experience. Reddy is happy to include bodily responses and gestures as 'emotives', as long as there is a degree of conscious decision-making in this process. Thus, if we label our emotion embarrassment and adjust our body to turn away as part of this script, then it becomes part of an emotive – an action that helps to produce our emotional experience. Reddy, however, excluded both blushing and tears from being 'emotives' as he saw them as unconscious responses, not purposeful attempts to direct our feeling. The problem with this claim, as Rob Boddice points out, is that blushing and crying are both shaped by culture.[3] Blushing is often associated with embarrassment, but not in all cultures; and what we are embarrassed by varies enormously by culture and occasionally across individuals, so that blushing occurs in different contexts in different times and places. Tears, as we explored in Chap. 3, are not dissimilar in this respect. Even if we accept that people do not consciously choose to blush (that it is an automatic response to a situation), blushing can direct our emotional response by indicating to us that we should feel embarrassed. Therefore, it has 'emotive-like' qualities in acting to mediate between bodily experience and cultural norms, encouraging us to align the remainder of our feeling to that emotional end.

If Reddy remains attached to this distinction between bodily experience and language, which emotives mediate, many historians do not and yet still find that his ideas have important uses. They consider the 'emotive' as a useful tool for explaining how emotion words come to be significant in directing emotional experience (something explored further in Chap. 6), and they find the idea of emotional regimes and refuges as valuable for highlighting how emotional norms come to cultural and political power and how they ultimately transform. Like many models of emotion, the mechanism by which people come to experience 'emotional suffering' is somewhat fuzzy. If it arises from the incapacity of language to fully represent bodily experience, why this is more challenging for some in a community than others is never quite clear. Yet, this is not significantly different from Rosenwein's slow and gradual transformations, where change arises as a part of historical conditions. Historical change, particularly when attached to norms, in all contexts can be difficult to explain.

APPLYING EMOTIONAL REGIMES

The concept of emotional regimes is distinct from the concepts of style and community because of its consideration of power. Many of the principles for applying the concept of emotional regimes are similar to other emotional methodologies, but extend analysis from an understanding of emotional norms to how they reinforce people's place within an institutional structure. Like for styles or communities, the first step is to identify emotion words, clusters and sequences, seeking to develop a model of what particular emotions incorporated in terms of gesture and action, where they happened, how they were valued or not by society and the consequences for not conforming. Part of this might be identifying emotion words as 'emotives', as terms that help produce emotion in line with cultural norms. Given that emotives describe moments where individuals try to navigate their feelings, historians might particularly attend to discussions of emotion where people try to figure out or explore their emotional experience (moments of confusion or distress). In practice, however, the procedure remains much the same as for other emotions research in that the historian still concerns themselves with identifying emotion words, their contexts and meanings.

Once a picture of the emotional culture or cultures has been developed, the historian has to determine their role within a wider society, culture or institution. Here the historian may need to decide the boundaries of their study – are they looking at a nation, a family, a school – and then seek to locate the emotion they have identified within that framework. Sometimes the discussion of emotion in the source itself may indicate whether it is a wider norm or subculture. Individuals might express their feeling in relation to other values or as a form of emotional suffering. However, sometimes the historian needs to step outside an individual source to locate it in the context they have chosen to study. Here we might ask who produced the source – was it the government or someone in a position of power? Was it an individual or interest group? We might ask who the intended audience of the source was – is it a private diary and so meant to be read by an individual or small group, or a political pamphlet aimed at wide circulation? We can also consider the history of the source material. Does it survive because the author was arrested and it forms part of a legal record? Was it a popular piece of literature owned by most homes?

This sort of information can help us work out what group our source material represents and, placing it into our knowledge of that environment, who might hold power and who was forming an emotional refuge. We should, of course, be careful here not to make assumptions about power. Sometimes the person formally 'in charge' might not set the emotional norms for a society and, indeed, this disjuncture may tell us something interesting about power dynamics. An example might be assuming that a headteacher determined the emotional culture of a school, but in fact this was largely shaped by powerful groups of students who had more power to 'punish' offenders through social exclusion. This might be especially pertinent at moments where there is a conflict between emotional or political regimes, and those with formal political power are losing control to another group.

Sometimes the emotional norm that we can identify is not that of the powerful but of an emotional refuge. This can be especially interesting as refuges have their own rules for emotional expression, and so while they can allow people a relief from emotional suffering, they also bind them into new systems of power. A study of a refuge may wish to identify how that community offered relief from suffering or outlets for emotional expression that were not otherwise available. But to do this may require knowledge of the wider culture not available to the historian, and so we may have to try and extrapolate how they were situating themselves in relation to an outsider community and what that might suggest for power relationships between them. The slave narratives below, read without any other sources, are a suggestive example of this.

Slave narratives, especially of free slaves – those who had escaped or been given their freedom – were popular during the nineteenth century, supported and published by abolitionists. They generally took the form of a life history and were designed to persuade the public of the wrongs of slavery and to promote the abolishment of slavery, particularly in the Americas and Caribbean. One of the challenges of producing these narratives was that the slave who was writing had to appear sympathetic to their audience, whilst also giving an account of a cruel system where behaving 'well' (as imagined by free White audiences) was not always tenable. Later, at the end of the nineteenth and into the early twentieth century, some people took oral testimonies from slaves as part of preserving their history as the last generation who formally lived under slavery, and these can be quite different in style. Those below, however, were produced to express the emotional and physical suffering of slaves to their owners and wider White society.

Writings by 'subalterns', or groups that had little formal power in society, that were aimed at wider audiences often had to perform a balancing act by writing in a language, often an emotional one when injustice was being described, that the powerful could understand, but which could also convey something of your own identity, needs and desires. To persuade another group to make changes, it could be useful to deploy stories and situations they would find particularly wrong, and to use an emotional vocabulary that they were familiar with. This did not mean lying, but rather selecting the types of situations that would get a response from your audience and avoiding those that they would find difficult to understand. Such writing also needed to humanise the writer so that the reader would make a connection with them. That might require describing situations and emotions that you both had in common to ensure that a connection could be made. A more ethically minded reader might suggest that this is a conservative approach to liberty, one that required the powerless to conform to emotional norms of the powerful to receive justice. And certainly some forms of liberatory politics have involved individuals or groups insisting that powerful groups expand their emotional repertoire to incorporate new emotions and new valuations of emotion. For people with very little power, like slaves, sometimes political freedom – the ending of slavery – was critical enough that other types of emotional freedom could wait. In a similar way, we can look at how African Americans in the twentieth century presented themselves as 'respectable' by borrowing middle-class clothes when campaigning for civil rights. At least in an Anglophone context, the powerful found it easier to extend rights to those that 'felt' like them.

One of the advantages of this for historians is that sources like slave narratives can tell us useful things not only about the emotional culture of slaves themselves (the emotional refuges they formed) but also of the dominant emotional culture who their writings were trying to target and persuade. Sometimes trying to identify the line between these two groups can be quite challenging (which was part of the point of this persuasive style of writing – 'we are just like you'); however, we should also remember that emotional refuges are formed from dominant culture, so they very often share similar values around emotion to each other anyway. Emotional refuges generally do not produce remarkably different emotional cultures, but rather more subtle shifts in norms of expression and the valuation of emotion. In many cases, like for slaves, what might be at stake was less a need for emotional liberty from dominant norms, but the right to exercise the same emotional freedoms as everyone else, to be recognised as fully human.

SLAVERY AND EMOTION

Emotion was critical to slavery in the nineteenth-century Americas. As noted in the previous chapter, the capacity to feel deeply was tied to ideas of civilisation and even humanity. The exclusion of Black people from human rights – the right not to be enslaved – was predicated on the idea that they were more primitive than others, a 'primitive' nature marked in a lack of emotional sophistication. This was not to suggest that Black people were thought to feel nothing, but that their passions and desires were more straightforward, more easily managed, than the White population. Many argued that Black people had little desire for liberty, happy to remain in bondage with a good master. This particular imagining of slave emotions as unsophisticated was deployed to exclude them from political rights.

Many slaveowners held emotional expectations of their slaves, particularly in public contexts (like the slave market), where they should appear cheerful and happy. Some even tied the happiness of their slaves to their productivity. Happy slaves worked harder and caused less problems; unhappy slaves ran away, worked slowly and caused rebellions. That slaves should be happy was expected to place certain limits on the slaveowner, who should restrain their violence and cruelty to encourage such feeling. Slaves that ran away, especially repeatedly, could be a matter of shame for slaveowners, suggesting they failed to properly manage their property. Yet, if cruelty should be avoided, that slaves were considered less sophisticated than White people meant that physical discipline was often considered the best tool for managing their behaviour, justifying violence and cruel treatment. Slavery placed expectations of emotional management on all members of the system.

The emotional 'style' of slavery in the nineteenth century was particularly tied to 'sentimentalism', a mode of expression that placed emotion above reason and particularly prized 'tenderness', pity and compassion. This may seem ironic for a regime that operated by refusing humanity to a group of people, but nonetheless slaveowners, abolitionists and slaves themselves all deployed sentimental language and tropes (reoccurring imagery) to explain both slavery and their individual experience of it. Slaveowners located their own actions as part of a paternalistic system where they cared for the child-like slave, denying them the capacity for a similar tender feeling. Abolitionists and slaves located the slaveowners as without feeling, hardened by their role in the system of slavery. They instead highlighted the emotional range and experience of the slave, their suffering under slavery (often marked by their mourning or displays of sadness) and their capacity to experience love, pleasure and other sentimental felt experiences.

Within abolitionist literature, as suggested above, people deployed a shared sentimental language to persuade their readership of the humanity of slaves. Yet, some studies have also sought to explore distinct slave emotional cultures, looking at how they produced families, found spaces for leisure and pleasure, or alternatively expressed their fear and anger either towards each other or towards their owners or other parts of society. Early works on slavery by historians in the mid-twentieth century, drawing on the idea that character and personality were shaped by environment, argued that perhaps slaves were emotionally stunted by the system of slavery, becoming apathetic or uncritically cheerful. This work was widely criticised by later writers who sought to explore how slaves continued their own traditional cultures, brought with them from their homelands and passed across generations, and how they developed new cultures as modes of resistance to the system of which they were part. They considered the 'cheerful' slave stereotype as not representative of 'authentic' feeling but of the emotional labour that slaves had to perform to keep their employers happy and to maintain their own safety.

These debates remain interesting to historians of emotion, not only because of the important political role of the history of slavery in teaching us about how racism works today, but because the history of emotions largely expects most people to conform to the emotional culture, or regime, that they live within. If distinct emotional communities form within a regime, their emotional register should generally diversify and enrich the operation of the regime by applying it to particular contexts, rather than resisting it. Emotional refuges should generally be rare, especially in more liberal political systems. Yet, slavery was a system where emotional suffering was produced by excluding people from the right to participate in the emotional regime of the dominant class. The emotional refuge of the slave was not necessarily emotionally distinct (although such refuges might exist too), but radical in their refusal to be excluded from the emotional regime of majority culture. Slavery helps us better understand how emotional and political systems intertwine in complex ways to produce emotional suffering.

NARRATIVISING SLAVERY

First-person accounts of slave lives published by abolitionist groups were popular in the nineteenth century as people tried to change White attitudes to slavery. The first account comes from the life of John Brown, an American slave who escaped to England. He tells of the first time he was sold and separated from his mother. The second narrative comes from William Brown. The excerpt describes a time in his life when he was an ex-slave, working for a slave trader. Here he describes a sale of slaves at a market. The final excerpt comes from a narrative by Mary Prince, who was a slave in the Caribbean. It describes the early part of her life. These sources can be read for what they tell us of both the emotional refuges of slavery and the emotional regime that dominated.

Begin by reading through the accounts, and summarising what they say. Why have these texts been produced? Who wrote and produced them? What do they have in common, and what is distinct to each piece? Can you identify repeating 'tropes' – that is, stories or imagery that take a similar form in each piece? Why do you think the authors placed an emphasis on these examples? Are there particular emotion words, concepts or clusters that appear in these texts? If these texts are designed to 'persuade', can you identify what techniques are being used to shape the attitudes and emotions of the reader? Are these compelling accounts? Why is it important that these texts are written in the first person? How does gender shape the expression of emotion in these texts?

Start to consider and identify the 'emotives'. What words are emotives in the texts? Why do you think that? Are there any other things in the texts that can act as emotives? If emotives 'do' things, what are they 'doing' in these texts? How do they help produce the emotional cultures found in these texts? How can we identify what emotional norms are dominant in these texts? Can they be used to develop a picture of the emotional norms of this community, and if so, is the community in question a refuge or a regime or something else?

What evidence is there of emotional suffering in these texts? Can we separate 'emotional suffering', that caused by a mismatch between personal feeling and the regime, from the political suffering caused by slavery? Are these slaves experiencing emotional suffering in Reddy's terms, or is their suffering of a different nature? If these are different, what would this suggest about the emotional culture of slaves? Are there suggestions in these texts that slaves might have different emotional norms from the dominant culture?

How does the model for emotional life offered by the slave accounts reinforce or undermine the political system of slavery? What does the existence of these pamphlets tell us about how this emotional regime understood emotions to work in shaping public opinion? Can we compare these with the texts in the last chapter? Are they performing a similar or different purpose?

1. John Brown, *Slave Life in Georgia: A Narrative of the Life, Sufferings, and Escape of John Brown, a Fugitive Slave, Now in England* (London, 1855), 13–16, 69–72.

Owing to a considerable rise in the price of cotton, there came a great demand for slaves in Georgia. One day a negro speculator named Starling Finney arrived at James Davis's place. He left his drove on the highway, in charge of one of his companions, and made his way up to our plantation, prospecting for negroes. It happened that James Davis had none that suited Finney, but being in want of money, as he was building a new house, and Finney being anxious for a deal, my master called me up and offered to sell me. I was then about or nearly ten years of age, and after some chaffering about terms, Finney agreed to purchase me by the pound.

How I watched them whilst they were driving this bargain! and how I speculated upon the kind of man he was who sought to buy me! His venomous countenance inspired me with mortal terror, and I almost felt the heavy thong of the great riding-whip he held in his hand, twisting round my shoulders. He was a large, tall fellow, and might have killed me easily with one blow from his huge fist. He had left his horse at the gate and when the bargain for me was struck, he went out and led him to the door, where he took the saddle off. I wondered what this was for, though suspicious that it had something to do with me, nor had I long to wait before I knew. A ladder was set upright against the end of the building outside, to one rong of which they made a stilyard fast. The first thing Finney did was to weigh his saddle, the weight of which he knew to see whether the stilyard was accurately adjusted. Having satisfied himself of this, a rope was brought, both ends of which were tied together so that it formed a large noose or loop. This was hitched over the hook of the stilyard, and I was seated in the loop. After I had been weighed, there was a deduction made for the rope. I do not recollect what I weighed, but the price I was sold for amounted to three hundred and ten dollars.

Within five minutes after, Finney paid the money, and I was marched off. I looked round and saw my poor mother stretching out her hands after me. She ran up, and overtook us, but Finney, who was behind me, and between me and my mother, would not let her approach, though she begged and prayed to be allowed to kiss me for the last time, and bid me good bye. I was so stupified with grief and fright, that I could not shed a tear, though my heart was bursting. At last we got to the gate, and I turned round to see whether I could not get a chance of kissing my mother. She saw me, and made a dart forward to meet me, but Finney gave me a hard push, which sent me spinning through the gate. He then slammed it to and shut it in my mother's face. That was the last time I ever saw her, nor do I know whether she is alive or dead at this hour.

We were in a lane now, about a hundred and fifty yards in length, and which led from the gate to the highway. I walked on before Finney, utterly unconscious of any thing. I seemed to have become quite bewildered. I was aroused from this state of stupor by seeing that we had reached the main road, and had come up with a gang of negroes, some of whom were hand-cuffed two and two, and fastened to a long chain running between the two ranks. There were also a good many women and children, but none of these were chained. The children seemed to be all above ten years of age, and I soon learnt that they had been purchased in different places, and were for the most part strangers to one another and to the negroes in the coffle. They were waiting for Finney to come up. I fell into the rank, and we set off on our journey to Georgia.

[He is sold several more times. He meets a man called John Glasgow, a free Black man, a sailor from England who had been captured and sold into slavery. Glasgow tells him many stories about his young family, and the freedom he enjoyed in England.]

My mind had long been made up to run away. I was constantly dwelling on what John Glasgow had told me about freedom, and England, and becoming a man. During my old master's lifetime, I had frequently hidden away in the wood and swamps; sometimes for a few days only; at others for a fortnight at a stretch; and once for a whole month. I used to sneak out at night from my hiding-place and steal corn, fruit, and such like. As long as it lasted, the release from the severe labour put upon me was quite grateful; and though I always got cruelly flogged on my return, the temptation to get a rest this way was too great to be resisted. It may be asked why I did not go right off when once I had made a start. I may as well tell the truth. I was frightened to take a long journey. I did not know the country, but I did know that if my master caught me and brought me back, I should get perhaps paddled or scourged nearly to death. I was, nevertheless, always on the look-out for a fair chance of escaping, and treasured up in my memory such scraps of information as I could draw out of the people that came to the plantation, especially the new hands. De Cator Stevens did not like to sell me, because I was too valuable to him. He used to say of me, that nothing came amiss to me; and in this, for once, he told the truth; for I may say, without unduly boasting, that at farming, at carpentering, and at any and all kinds of labour, I was a match for any two hands he could bring against me. In fact, I could and used to do two men's work, when I returned from my lying-out. At such times I could only compare myself to a man gone lunatic.

Knowing Stevens would not sell me, and having made up my mind to suffer any amount of flogging, I grew defiant of my master, but I determined I would be killed in defending myself if he should use me too hard. I also took to studying his countenance, until I became so accustomed to its expression and to his ways, that I could always tell whether he intended mischief. At such times I would get out of the way. The older I grew, and the stronger, the less fearful I became; and then I noticed that my master got frightened of me, lest I should run away. All this, however, did not save my poor back; but whenever Stevens wanted to spite me, he would not ask the men to hold me, for fear I should kill them, but used to creep up very slily, and hit me unawares, or throw sticks, chunks, and big stones at me, which sometimes hit and hurt me, and sometimes missed me and injured another. All this I bore. I wanted to get a clear start, for my mind was bent upon making tracks for England, which I fancied was not very far away. So I put up with the floggings and the ill-usage, and bided my time. ...

At length I determined to be off. John Glasgow had been given away about two years before, to Stevens' son John. When he went I lost my only friend. But all he had told me rested on my mind. My whole thoughts dwelt upon England, and as things seemed to be getting worse with me, I considered the time was come for me to make a bold start for liberty.

2. *Narrative of William W. Brown, an American Slave. Written by Himself* (London, 1850), 44–46.

The next day we proceeded to New Orleans, and put the gang in the same negro-pen which we occupied before. In a short time the planters came flocking to the pen to purchase slaves. Before the slaves were exhibited for sale, they were dressed and driven out into the yard. Some were set to dancing, some to jumping, some to singing, and some to playing cards. This was done to make them appear cheerful and happy. My business was to see that they were placed in those situations before the arrival of the purchasers, and I have often set them to dancing when their cheeks were wet with tears. As slaves were in good demand at that time, they were soon all disposed of, and we again set out for St. Louis.

On our arrival, Mr. Walker purchased a farm five or six miles from the city. He had no family, but made a housekeeper of one of his female slaves. Poor Cynthia! I knew her well. She was a quadroon, and one of the most beautiful women I ever saw. She was a native of St. Louis, and bore an irreproachable character for virtue and propriety of conduct. Mr. Walker bought her for the New Orleans market, and took her down with him on one of the trips that I made with him. Never shall I forget the circumstances of that voyage! On the first night that we were on board the steamboat, he directed me to put her into a state-room he had provided for her, apart from the other slaves. I had seen too much of the workings of slavery not to know what this meant. I accordingly watched him into the state-room, and listened to hear what passed between them. I heard him make his base offers, and her reject them. He told her that if she would accept his vile proposals, he would take her back with him to St. Louis, and establish her as his housekeeper on his farm. But if she persisted in rejecting him, he would sell her as a field hand on the worst plantation on the river. Neither threats nor bribery prevailed, however, and he retired, disappointed of his prey.

3. *The History of Mary Prince, a West Indian Slave. Related by Herself,* 3 ed. (London: F. Westley and A. H. Davis, 1831), 1–4.

I was born at Brackish-Pond, in Bermuda, on a farm belonging to Mr. Charles Myners. My mother was a household slave; and my father, whose name was Prince, was a sawyer belonging to Mr. Trimmingham, a ship-builder at Crow-Lane. When I was an infant, old Mr. Myners died, and there was a division of the slaves and other property among the family. I was bought along with my mother by old Captain Darrel, and given to his grandchild, little Miss Betsey Williams. Captain Williams, Mr. Darrel's son-in-law, was master of a vessel which traded to several places in America and the West Indies, and he was seldom at home long together.

Mrs. Williams was a kind-hearted good woman, and she treated all her slaves well. She had only one daughter, Miss Betsey, for whom I was purchased, and who was about my own age. I was made quite a pet of by Miss Betsey, and loved her very much. She used to lead me about by the hand, and call me her little nigger. This was the happiest period of my life; for I was too young to understand rightly my condition as a slave, and too thoughtless and full of spirits to look forward to the days of toil and sorrow.

My mother was a household slave in the same family. I was under her own care, and my little brothers and sisters were my play-fellows and companions. My mother had several fine children after she came to Mrs. Williams, three girls and two boys. The tasks given out to us children were light, and we used to play together with Miss Betsey, with as much freedom almost as if she had been our sister.

My master, however, was a very harsh, selfish man; and we always dreaded his return from sea. His wife was herself much afraid of him; and, during his stay at home, seldom dared to shew her usual kindness to the slaves. He often left her, in the most distressed circumstances, to reside in other female society, at some place in the West Indies of which I have forgot the name. My poor mistress bore his ill-treatment with great patience, and all her slaves loved and pitied her. I was truly attached to her, and, next to my own mother, loved her better than any creature in the world. My obedience to her commands was cheerfully given: it sprung solely from the affection I felt for her, and not from fear of the power which the white people's law had given her over me.

I had scarcely reached my twelfth year when my mistress became too poor to keep so many of us at home; and she hired me out to Mrs. Pruden, a lady who lived about five miles off, in the adjoining parish, in a large house near the sea. I cried bitterly at parting with my dear mistress and Miss Betsey, and when I kissed my mother and brothers and sisters, I thought my young heart would break, it pained me so. But there was no help; I was forced to go. Good Mrs. Williams comforted me by saying that I should still be near the home I was about to quit, and might come over and see her and my kindred whenever I could obtain leave of absence from Mrs. Pruden. A few hours after this I was taken to a strange house, and found myself among strange people. This separation seemed a sore trial to me then; but oh! 'twas light, light to the trials I have since endured! – 'twas nothing – nothing to be mentioned with them; but I was a child then, and it was according to my strength. ...

At this time Mrs. Williams died. I was told suddenly of her death, and my grief was so great that, forgetting I had the baby in my arms, I ran away directly to my poor mistress's house; but reached it only in time to see the corpse carried out. Oh, that was a day of sorrow, a heavy day! All the slaves cried. My mother cried and lamented her sore; and I (foolish creature!) vainly entreated them to bring my dear mistress back to life. I knew nothing rightly about death then, and it seemed a hard thing to bear. When I thought about my mistress I felt as if the world was all gone wrong; and for many days and weeks I could think of nothing else. I returned to Mrs. Pruden's; but my sorrow was too great to be comforted, for my own dear mistress was always in my mind. Whether in the house or abroad, my thoughts were always talking to me about her.

I staid at Mrs. Pruden's about three months after this; I was then sent back to Mr. Williams to be sold. Oh, that was a sad sad time! I recollect the day well. Mrs. Pruden came to me and said, "Mary, you will have to go home directly;

your master is going to be married, and he means to sell you and two of your sisters to raise money for the wedding." Hearing this I burst out a crying, though I was then far from being sensible of the full weight of my misfortune, or of the misery that waited for me. ... I left Mrs. Pruden's, and walked home with a heart full of sorrow. The idea of being sold away from my mother and Miss Betsey was so frightful, that I dared not trust myself to think about it. We had been bought of Mr. Myners, as I have mentioned, by Miss Betsey's grandfather, and given to her, so that we were by right her property, and I never thought we should be separated or sold away from her. ...

Oh dear! I cannot bear to think of that day, it is too much. It recalls the great grief that filled my heart, and the woeful thoughts that passed to and fro through my mind, whilst listening to the pitiful words of my poor mother, weeping for the loss of her children. I wish I could find words to tell you all I then felt and suffered. The great God above alone knows the thoughts of the poor slave's heart, and the bitter pains which follow such separations as these. All that we love taken away from us – Oh, it is sad, sad! and sore to be borne! – I got no sleep that night for thinking of the morrow; and dear Miss Betsey was scarcely less distressed. She could not bear to part with her old playmates, and she cried sore and would not be pacified.

The black morning at length came; it came too soon for my poor mother and us. Whilst she was putting on us the new osnaburgs in which we were to be sold, she said, in a sorrowful voice, (I shall never forget it!) "See, I am shrouding my poor children; what a task for a mother!" ... Our mother, weeping as she went, called me away with the children Hannah and Dinah, and we took the road that led to Hamble Town, which we reached about four o'clock in the afternoon. We followed my mother to the market-place, where she placed us in a row against a large house, with our backs to the wall and our arms folded across our breasts. I, as the eldest, stood first, Hannah next to me, then Dinah; and our mother stood beside, crying over us. My heart throbbed with grief and terror so violently, that I pressed my hands quite tightly across my breast, but I could not keep it still, and it continued to leap as though it would burst out of my body. But who cared for that? Did one of the many by-standers, who were looking at us so carelessly, think of the pain that wrung the hearts of the negro woman and her young ones? No, no! They were not all bad, I dare say, but slavery hardens white people's hearts towards the blacks; and many of them were not slow to make their remarks upon us aloud, without regard to our grief though their light words fell like cayenne on the fresh wounds of our hearts. Oh those white people have small hearts who can only feel for themselves.

CONCLUSION

The three slave narratives above use a variety of emotion words, or emotives, to depict the experience of slavery. John Brown's experience is perhaps particularly interesting for a discussion of 'emotives', given his explicit consideration of his confusion and the time it took to name his feeling. He lays out his emotional journey and how he attempts to manage his feeling within an emotional system that refused him the right to feel. This was a description of emotion designed to suggest his emotional depth and complexity, as well as heightening the terrible impact of being sold away from his family. Describing himself as in a 'stupor' also allowed him to suggest that, while slaves did not always display emotion on being sold, nonetheless the impact was significant. A similar claim can be seen in William Prince's account of the slave market where he juxtaposes the forced cheerfulness expected of slaves with the tears on their face. This was an account that evidenced not just a cruel regime that denied slaves the right to express what they felt, but the capacity of slaves to live complex emotional lives.

Gender also appears to have mattered in these accounts, where female slaves – such as John Brown's mother – have more freedom to express grief or pain openly than men. Mary Prince's narrative contains considerably more emotion words – 'sorrow', 'grief', 'woeful' – than the other accounts, although the overall function of her narrative is to provide a similar account of the experience of slavery as her male counterparts. Gender also functions in these accounts to direct the sympathy of the reader. Women and also children, associated with innocence and in need of protection, are deployed in all of these accounts to reinforce the inhumanity of a system that increases their suffering. We might say that women, like Cynthia, or the queue of children who had been purchased alongside John Brown, become 'emotives', emotional signs designed to direct and produce feeling for the reader. We can see other similar ideas functioning similarly in these texts, such as the idea of 'home', as a romantic site of belonging that slavery destroys, or the act of selling a human as a moment of particular immorality, and so horror.

Having begun to understand this emotional culture, we can come to identify some features of the emotional regime of slavery. Reading against the grain, we might suggest that slaves were expected not to display emotion at distressing events and were even expected to appear cheerful and playful. We might also note that, despite the exclusion of slaves from a right to feeling, the use of these pamphlets as political rhetoric suggests that the dominant emotional regime generally did celebrate highly emotional accounts of personal experience and interior life, and that they required such emotion to make a human connection with others. These accounts affirm the significance of sentimentalism as the emotional regime of slavery.

We might also be able to identify some emotional refuges within these narratives. That individuals felt strong emotions in response to their circumstances, even if their opportunities to display these feelings on the body before the White community were limited, may have acted as a form of refuge within this wider system. Other slaves recognised each other's humanity, even if their masters did not. The emphasis on family, especially mother and child, and friends is also indicative of the capacity of loving relationships to act as emotional refuges, heightening the tragedy of removal. Finally, we might consider John Brown's various short-term escape attempts as sites of emotional refuge, a period away from the system of slavery, that allowed him to recoup and recover before he returned to his suffering. If these emotional refuges perhaps helped maintain the larger regime of slavery, in helping people find ways of coping within it, they may also have contributed to its formal dissolution, offering a space for feeling that allowed slaves to ultimately make a human connection with the White community, and to use that to demand freedom.

FURTHER READING

Emotional Regimes

*Boddice, Rob. *The History of Emotions*, 59–83. Manchester: Manchester University Press, 2018.

Garrido, Sandra, and Jane Davidson. 'Emotional Regimes Reflected in a Popular Ballad: Perspectives on Gender, Love and Protest in "Scarborough Fair".' *Musicology Australia* 39 (2016): 65–78.

Meek, Jeff. 'Risk! Pleasure! Affirmation! Navigating Queer Urban Spaces in Twentieth-Century Scotland.' In *The Routledge History Handbook of Gender & the Urban Experience*, eds. Deborah Simonton et al., 385–96. London: Routledge, 2017.

Plamper, Jan. 'The History of Emotions: A Interview with William Reddy, Barbara Rosenwein, and Peter Stearns.' *History and Theory* 49, no. 2 (2010): 237–65.

*Reddy, William M. *The Navigation of Feeling: A Framework for the History of Emotions*. Cambridge: Cambridge University Press, 2001.

Rosenwein, Barbara. 'Worrying About Emotions in History.' *American Historical Review* 107, no. 3 (2002): 821–45.

Rosenwein, Barbara. 'Theories of Change in the History of Emotions.' In *A History of Emotions, 1200–1800*, ed. Jonas Liliequist, 7–20. London: Routledge, 2012.

Singh, Jyotsna G. '"Th'Expense of Spirit in a Waste of Shame": Mapping the "Emotional Regime" of Shakespeare's Sonnets.' In *A Companion to Shakespeare's Sonnets*, ed. Michael Schoenfeldt, 277–89. Oxford: Blackwell, 2010.

Slavery and Emotion

Dwyer, Erin. 'Mastering Emotions: The Emotional Politics of Slavery.' Doctoral Dissertation, Harvard University, 2012.

Eustace, Nicole. *1812: War and the Passions of Patriotism*. University Park: University of Pennsylvania Press, 2012.

Festa, Lynn. *Sentimental Figures of Empire in Eighteenth-Century Britain and France*. Baltimore: Johns Hopkins, 2006.

Hartman, Saidiya. *Scenes of Subjection: Terror, Slavery, and Self-Making in Nineteenth-Century America*. Oxford: Oxford University Press, 1997.

Lamb-Brooks, Benjamin. *Angry Abolitionists and the Rhetoric of Slavery: Moral Emotions in Social Movements*. New York: Palgrave, 2016.

Lussana, Sergio. '"No Band of Brothers Could Be More Loving": Enslaved Male Homosociality, Friendship, and Resistance in the Antebellum American South.' *Journal of Social History* 46, no. 4 (2013): 872–95.

Lussana, Sergio. *My Brother Slaves: Friendship, Masculinity and Resistance in the Antebellum South*. Lexington: University Press of Kentucky, 2016.

Mallipeddi, Ramesh. *Spectacular Suffering: Witnessing Slavery in the Eighteenth-Century British Atlantic*. Charlottesville: University of Virginia Press, 2016.

Palmer, Jennifer L. *Intimate Bonds: Family and Slavery in the French Atlantic*. Pennsylvania: University of Pennsylvania Press, 2016.

Sharples, Jason T. 'Discovering Slave Conspiracies: New Fears of Rebellion and Old Paradigms of Plotting in Seventeenth-Century Barbados.' *American Historical Review* 120, no. 3 (2015): 811–43.

Sharples, Jason T. 'Slavery and Fear.' In *Oxford Bibliographies in Atlantic History*, ed. Trevor Burnard. Oxford: Oxford University Press, 2018. www.oxfordbibliographies.com/view/document/obo-9780199730414/obo-9780199730414-0308.xml (Accessed 9 September 2019).

Stearns, Peter N., and Jan Lewis, eds. *An Emotional History of the United States*. New York: New York University Press, 1998.

Woods, Michael E. *Emotional and Sectional Conflict in the Antebellum United States*. New York: Cambridge University Press, 2014.

Woods, Michael E. 'Politics and Changing Views of Jealousy in the Antebellum United States.' In *Emotions and Social Change: Historical and Sociological Perspectives*, eds. David Lemmings and Ann Brookes, 156–72. New York: Routledge, 2014.

6 Practices and Performances

Practice and performance theories offer two different ways of exploring the relationship between nature and culture that moves past seeing them as working in binary opposition. They are slightly different theories, which will be explored below, but they have similar effects when applied by historians of emotions to their sources. Practice theory as applied to emotions was devised by Monique Scheer, who built upon Pierre Bourdieu's concept of *habitus*. Performance theory as used in the history of emotions is not associated with a particular thinker, but draws on a scholarly tradition that includes the philosopher John L. Austin, the sociologist Erving Goffman and the gender theorist Judith Butler. The work of many of these theorists also underpins William Reddy's 'emotives'. They are increasingly important ideas because not only do they move beyond the nature/culture divide, they are compatible with many of the other theories discussed in this book. Therefore, many historians now combine practice theory with the concept of emotional communities or performance theory with emotional regimes. This chapter explores these ideas, looking at how they are applied to historical sources. It has a particular focus on how we might use these ideas with material culture sources, especially those associated with religious devotions like relics.

PRACTICES AND PERFORMANCES

To understand how both practice and performance theory work, it can be useful to think of the world as consisting of a set of resources that the human uses to produce the 'self', where the self is an individual person who can self-consciously reflect on who and what they are. These resources include the human body, its specificities (like sex organs or the absence of a limb), clothing, furniture, books, ornaments and other material goods, language and words, and ideas or discourses, the big concepts that help us make sense of the world. The latter might include 'the law', as a set of rules that shape social life, or cultural norms about gender that suggest men should not express emotion.

Some of the philosophy that underpins the discussion we have been having across this book categorised these resources into two groups – the 'material' (like the body and furniture) and 'representational' (like language and discourses). This division can sometimes also be called nature and culture. As we have seen in our consideration of the physical experience of emotion versus how we express it, some groups think that the material is most important in shaping human experience, and that language and discourses are just a gloss we place upon it to help us manage the material and the relations of power it enables; others argue that representation or language is primary as 'the material' is only meaningful through human perception. The problem with this debate is that we spend a lot of time worrying about two sides of the same equation without finding any solution.

A number of theorists have instead tried to find ways to think about the relationship between the material and representation that explain how they might work together. William Reddy's idea of an 'emotive' is one of these. As we explored in the last chapter, an emotive is a word that is not just 'representational' – a sign that stands in for a material thing – but a word that does something – it produces emotion by shaping both our understanding of our experience and our bodily feeling of that emotion. Practice theorists and performance theorists are similarly trying to provide explanations of how the material and representational work together, if in slightly different ways from each other. They are trying to explain how all the 'resources' described above are used together by humans to produce the self, including emotion as an experience of the individual.

To do this, they decided to move away from the idea that there are 'emotional rules' or norms on the one hand and the individual experience of emotion on the other. There is a suggestion of this in Rosenwein's idea that there is not a distinction between emotion words and the emotional experiences they shape. This is not because emotional rules do not exist. Rather, practice and performance theorists both think that we should focus on how individuals 'do' emotion in particular situations. A situation can include a physical environment – a workplace or sports arena – but also a relationship, like a marriage, or even within a written form, like a letter or persuasive pamphlet. Within each situation, the individual draws on their 'resources' (their body, their cultural beliefs, their typewriter) to produce 'the self', including their experience of emotion. Now it could be that one of the resources they draw on in that situation are the emotional rules that exist in their culture, but how they are deployed by the individual will likely vary according to the specific situation and in relation to their other resources.

An example of this might be a man in a public house who is aggravated by another customer calling him 'fat'. Within the cultural norms for masculinity and the expression of emotion in his culture, by rights this man should punch the customer. However, the customer is physically very large and dangerous-looking, and so the man also feels fear and decides not to act on his anger but to make a joke of the situation, trying to direct this encounter into an outcome other than violence. The customer, appreciating this effort, may also move emotional registers from enemy to friend, offering to buy the man he insulted a drink. In the meantime, the watching public, drinking in the pub, also shift in their emotions from anxious – anticipating potential violence – to relaxed, able to enjoy the remainder of their evening. Lots of different things went into creating this emotional encounter. There were a range of cultural discourses relating to codes of masculinity and also emotional expressions brought into play. There were assessments made of each other's bodies, their own and the environment in which the encounter happened (was this an appropriate place to have a fight?). These men also deployed recognised social rituals – sharing alcohol – to try and shift this emotional encounter to a more positive outcome. The experience might have been quite different if the man who was insulted had thought that he should have behaved violently and punched the customer. His anger may have led to other people fleeing the scene in fright, or picking sides and getting involved. The outcome may have been the death of one of the protagonists, rather than making a new friend.

Emotional rules might have been deployed in this fight, but they were carefully managed and adapted to the circumstances. Rather what mattered was the combination of bodies, place and cultural ideas brought together by an individual who made a set of assessments about the situation and how to respond. Importantly, this emotional experience was not just one of rational thought, but embodiment. Bodies mattered here, both in shaping the assessment of whether violence was appropriate (yikes, that's a dangerous-looking man!), and because their bodies experienced emotion as feeling. Anger and fear were not just ideas but adaptive responses to the scenario in which they were placed. Moreover these emotions were not just passive responses to reasoned assessments of the situation, but helped to direct judgement – feeling fear at the size of an assailant directed the man towards a non-violent response. Practice and performance theorists ultimately suggest that, while ideas or rules about emotions are important to shaping human behaviour, it is not until we are in situations that emotions really exist, and therefore to understand them, we should focus on analysing such situations.

Moreover, they suggest that, by understanding emotions (and indeed the self) as things that are produced in situations, we can also avoid worrying about distinctions between the material and the representational. Rather they suggest that in a particular situation the human deploys all their 'resources' – their body, property, beliefs, values – together, each acting with the others to produce the situation that is emotional experience. In this situation, no resource comes before the others; they all work together to create emotional experience. Because every situation is different, and because each person has a different set of resources, each experience of emotion is unique or individual, whilst still being 'socially constituted', shaped by our cultural education and historical context.

Practice theorists describe this use of resources as a set of 'practices', things people do to produce the self, emotions or other phenomena. They particularly emphasise how the world is made through a 'dialectic', a back and forth, between social structure (that is, the big systems like economy, law, religion, but also ideas about race, gender, the body) and human agency, that is the ways that humans apply these structures in their everyday experience. Neither should take primacy over the other. The main theorist to apply these ideas to understanding of emotion is Monique Scheer, who especially draws on Bourdieu's idea of *habitus*. She argues that emotions are effectively produced through emotional practices, but that these practices are performed by bodies which are products of their time and place. Effectively the body and its responses are a product of education, habits that have become so engrained that they are experienced not just in our decision-making but also in our muscles, physical reflexes and feeling. As a result, the body is a cultural product and our embodied experience reflects the way our material body and our cultural education reciprocally shape each other and are formed together.

Performance theorists place more emphasis on the instability of the self – and so of emotion. They emphasise that, in every situation, we are effectively a bundle of potential that 'becomes' through our performance. Social structures or categories – like gender or an emotion like anger – come into existence because people repeatedly perform in the same way to enable an effect. Anger becomes a recognisable category as people perform it in the same way over and over. Because we do these performances regularly, they come to feel natural and biological. Like with practice theory, our performances do not exist outside of our cultural context, but norms and ideas are deployed as part of the performance to help make it intelligible to ourselves and others. Our performances are always social – produced with other people and culture – as well as individual. Like for practice theorists, these norms are learned from childhood, so can be performed unthinkingly. However, at times, individuals may wish to subvert or resist such norms and adapt their performances accordingly to enable different effects. The man who chooses to joke, rather than punch the customer who insulted him, might be considered in this context. Not unlike an emotional style, performance theorists allow greater space for individuals to negotiate their personal emotional experience by adopting or rejecting particular styles or norms. Yet, as Reddy's model would suggest, alternative performances of emotion may entail emotional suffering if society does not welcome such a presentation of self.

APPLYING PRACTICE AND PERFORMANCE THEORY

Practice and performance theory both emphasise the importance of studying emotions in particular situations, attending to not just emotion words but also bodies, gestures, expressions, relationships and the environments in which they are negotiated. Emotional experience is made up of the entire performance, not just one part such as an emotion word. Scheer suggests that there are four types of emotional practices, which historians can identify: mobilising, naming, communicating and regulating. We 'mobilise' emotions when we use emotional rituals or practices, like listening to music or taking drugs, to try and shape our own, or others', emotions. Therefore we can look to identify situations where people are trying to mobilise their emotions or those of others. This could include identifying how the pamphlets in the last chapter deployed emotional stories to shape public opinion, or it might involve exploring how religious rituals were designed to move the sorrowing sinner towards joy. The practice of 'naming' emotions helps to organise our experience of emotion; this is the same principle as Reddy's concept of the 'emotive' and can be looked for in a similar manner by identifying emotion words or words that do emotional work.

Communicating practices are when we perform or display emotion to others, an act that can be more or less successful. This might involve expressing emotion on the face and body, as well as making statements about our feeling. A historian might therefore wish to look for descriptions of emotions being expressed through bodily behaviours, like those discussed in the South American literature in Chap. 4, or even to assess the love letters in Chap. 2 as a form of communicative practice. 'Regulating' practices are a reference to the emotional norms communities develop to guide emotional behaviour, and can be charted as a 'style' and subcultures in a similar manner to that explored in previous chapters. Scheer notes that, while we can look for evidence of emotional practices, this is mainly an analytical lens that we bring to source material; past people will not generally identify their behaviour as an emotional practice or performance. They may not even mention any emotions involved.

Performance theorists have a similar focus in their analysis of source material. Like Scheer, they place particular emphasis on what people are doing and the contexts in which they are doing it. When the goal is understanding emotion, historians should look not only for emotion words, but how bodies are described, their gestures and actions; for discussions of mental states and metaphors designed to express interior experiences; for interpersonal exchanges that suggest care, concern or its absence; for rituals designed to transform, exchange or communicate emotion. The latter might include everyday rituals that individuals participate in, from religious practices to small acts of love (making the morning tea) or significant political rituals, such as those performed by monarchs to express their happiness or displeasure to their subjects.

Like much historical research, this might be done by looking for descriptions of people and their behaviours written by contemporaries or depicted in art and literature. Similarly to our exploration of South American phrenology, we may then wish to analyse these gestures and behaviours through the cultural lens of the period, recognising whether they symbolise emotion or something more complicated like morality or a cultural trope, such as the sorrowful widow. It can be tempting to imagine that contemporary descriptions of the emotional body, produced by scientists and doctors, are somehow 'truer' or more realistic accounts of emotion than these past depictions. Yet, in their own insistence that emotions are simply biological, or biocultural, they too reflect a particular historical perspective, evidencing our contemporary concerns and understandings of the body. Instead, we might ask what do such accounts 'do' – what kinds of knowledges do they produce about emotion and the body; what kind of moral messages do they transmit to the reader; what kind of impacts do such accounts have on the world? If we believe that a particular description of emotion or the body is intended to represent real events (like a journalist's account of a courtroom), we may also consider how they were interpreted by others in the account (how did the jury respond to a witness weeping on the stand) and by the journalist describing the scene (did they portray the weeping witness sympathetically or not). From this we can build a picture of how the emotional events described were understood to work and what emotion did within that situation.

As noted in Chap. 1, sources themselves are also important pieces of evidence for their material functions, as well as what they say or describe. Regardless of what it said, the love letter played an important role in courtship rituals as an object that stood in for an absent loved one. Material culture objects – everything from items of clothing to furniture to buildings to tools and weapons – that do not have writing on them can nonetheless provide important evidence about how people did things in the past. Sometimes an object might contain marks that suggest it was used as part of an emotional practice or performance, such as a love heart carved into a spoon or a couple's initials stitched onto a tablecloth. Other times the 'emotional' potential of an object might be suggested by the material it is made from, perhaps elaborate jewels or expensive cloth, and its survival over time (suggesting that it mattered enough for someone to keep). This approach has shortcomings as it tends to lead us to prize expensive or ritual objects over everyday items. Yet, toys, trinkets, gifts and token inheritances can play an important role in the emotional lives of individuals, as symbols of love, friendship, family or ephemeral traces of an important event, like the ticket of a concert. Even items that do not have considerable personal significance can shape our emotional lives, such as the way clothes might mark people as working class and so limit who they might fall in love with or how they were treated by a middle-class businessowner.

Analysing material objects and places can sometimes feel more challenging than written texts, because we have less formal education in translating and interpreting material goods and as information that might help us do this can be harder to access than dictionaries or other written texts. To begin analysing material goods, we might attend closely to what it is made of, marks of usage and wear, its history and why it survived over time; we might compare it with similar items and their provenances, developing a history of how they were made, by whom and for what purpose. Ideally, especially for a history of emotion, an understanding of how it was used – what people did with it, where, when and why – can give us access to a 'situation' or 'performance' to analyse. Sometimes, all that survives is the object, and here we try to use the details we have – such as marks of wear and usage – to develop a story about how people used it and what that might suggest to us about the performances or practices of which it was a part.

Like other emotion sources, developing a robust understanding of the operation of emotion generally requires using multiple sources together to try and build a rich picture of an emotional culture and the contexts in which that culture came to be performed. One of the advantages of practice and performance theories however is that, in attending to the whole of the performance as part of emotion, we have multiple entry points into what we want to understand – the body, the word, material culture, architecture, landscape. While we might only have a partial view, because the source material only gives access to a single part of the full performance, nonetheless the historian has a greater chance of some sort of source material surviving that can give us access to an emotional performance.

MATERIAL CULTURE AND RELIGIOUS HISTORY

Objects of all sorts played a significant role in early modern European religious practice. Roman Catholics used a rich array of material goods to decorate their churches. They painted their walls in bright colours with scenes from the bible, saints' lives, or which provided moral messages. They enclosed their stonework within precious metals or rich material, covered their altars in cloth and utilised an array of religious objects – relics of dead saints, valuable communion cups, beautifully illuminated manuscripts – as part of their regular devotions. Both the church itself, perhaps a cathedral with sweeping balustrades and stained glass, and devotional objects were actively used to aid the practice of the faith, to help Christians ready themselves for the afterlife. The Christian entering a cathedral, through the scale of the building, the use of light and candles, should feel uplifted, taken closer to heaven, perhaps awed as they would become in the presence of God. Spiritual transformation was recognised as an inherently emotional processes; individuals were to sorrow with Mary, to empathise with Christ during his crucifixion, to find joy in access to the divine. Faith was felt, and emotional objects were deployed as part of devotional rituals to enable Christians to experience the emotions that would purify the soul and bind them to their spiritual communities.

During the Reformation, many of these objects were destroyed or converted to alternative uses. Altar cloths were given to the poor as blankets; rich fabrics were transformed into clothes; and devotional objects brought into homes for everyday purposes.[1] In their transformation from sacred to everyday objects, the emotional impacts evolved for new contexts and perhaps were used in new performances. Yet, sometimes, the history of their uses may have lingered as a form of memory, shaping how people used them or responded to them, or even as material marks on the item itself, such as scratches to obliterate a particular saint or the seams where a cloth has been unpicked and remade. Memories, and so affective investments, in objects may have even heightened over time as some were rescued and returned to religious use or taken into private collections or museums. As items considered to be important parts of our heritage, religious objects may produce a new set of emotions again, no longer directing people towards God but to a sense of themselves as part of a longer lineage or national history. Such objects might then provoke patriotism, or alternatively trouble our sense of the past and identity, as we reflect on an object's various uses over the centuries.

Here we might reflect on how someone would have encountered a particular object. Very often historians access early modern devotional objects through a museum, observing them through a glass wall or (if fortunate) gingerly holding them as they inspect them for their research. But when used for devotional purposes, objects were often handled repeatedly. Indeed, the primary purpose of many of them was as a form of memory aid, but where memory was enabled through the senses, primarily touch but perhaps also smell and sight. Relics of the lives of saints, stored in reliquaries that allowed them to be handled by individuals or groups, directed the Christian to reflect on the saint's sacrifice; when used as part of significant rituals, they might be accompanied by group prayers, songs, processions, incense and other corporeal experiences. More everyday objects, like rosary beads, might have been used for private devotion, but nonetheless worked to mobilise memory and shape emotion through being touched. Each bead on the rosary stood for a prayer; the devotee used them as a physical guide to as they worked through a sequence of devotions.

Objects draw our attention to emotion, and emotional transformation, as something enabled through the body, not just as internal feeling but through gestures, actions and the use of material goods. We can also see this in a number of rituals designed to enable social relationships or commitments. The kiss of peace was a ritual where medieval people exchanged kisses to indicate the end of a feud; today we might shake hands instead, a less intimate act but still involving physical touch. Holy Communion involved the taking of bread and wine in a ritual designed to form the Christian community, something then replicated in hospitality rituals in secular contexts. Even now, many European cultures share alcohol at events where people are introduced to each other. Bodies not only experience emotion as feeling but could be mobilised to enable particular feeling. Material goods that brought body and memory together seemed to be particularly effective at generating emotion. In turn, such emotion gave significance to such items, 'sticking' as Sara Ahmed might say, and ensuring their significance to people across the centuries.

RELIGIOUS MATERIAL CULTURE

Medieval and early modern Europeans practised their faith using a wide array of material culture practices. Devotion to God – something that was expected to be an embodied and encompassing feeling – was enabled using a range of devotional items with different purposes and functions. Consider the items below. Describe the items and their key features. Do we know what they are? How might they have been used? Are there marks of wear on the item that suggest how they may have been handled or used? Do we know when such marks might have appeared (at what point in an object's history)? Looking at what the object is made from, what do we learn about its value, both economic and emotional? Are there any distinct features or decoration that might help us understand the purpose of the object? Do we have any contextual information – any history of the object – that can tell us something of its use? If not, can we contrast it with similar objects and use these comparisons to help us analyse it? Having now built a database of information about the object, in what kind of situations and rituals might it have been used? Would these situations have been emotional, and what do we mean by that? Would the object help generate or transform emotion? Could it have been involved in emotional practices in less direct ways? How might we feel confident about that analysis? What other sources could we use to help affirm our knowledge of the 'situation' it was used in and its emotional effects? How necessary is such contextualisation? Can we work with an object or objects alone to construct emotional performances?

Religious Objects

Christians used an array of religious objects to enable their faith in everyday life. Figure 6.1 is a set of rosary beads. These came in many designs and were used to help count the repetitive prayers spoken during the rosary. This set focuses on images of death and the last judgement, a reminder to Christians of

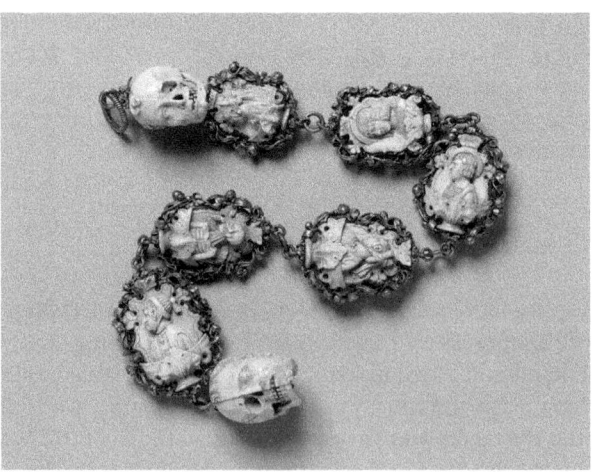

Figure 6.1 Rosary, German ca. 1500–1525, Ivory, silver and partially gilded mounts, The Metropolitan Museum of Art, New York

the importance of salvation and the afterlife.[2] Figure 6.2 is a pilgrimage badge.[3] Many medieval and early modern Christians went on pilgrimages to places of spiritual significance – holy wells, major cathedrals, Jerusalem. At these sites, they could purchase badges made from an array of materials and at different prices. This steel example features the three Marys (Magdalene, the Virgin, and St Mary of Egypt). They were often thought to have magical powers or bring luck. It was found in a river, a popular place to dispose of these items as part of ritual and superstitious practices. Figure 6.3 is a similar object, but this time shaped as a cross with symbols that signify both St Zachariah and St Benedict.[4] Each letter on the cross formed part of an 'acrostic', corresponding to a particular prayer. A Christian was expected to see each letter and remember the associated prayer, saying them in order. In this case, the prayers were designed as protection against diseases like the plague. Figure 6.4 is a pendant reliquary featuring an image of the Angel Gabriel visiting Mary to tell her that she will be the mother of Christ.[5] A reliquary is an object designed to hold a relic, such as part of the body of a saint or Christ, or similar spiritual item. A pendant

Figure 6.2 Pilgrimage souvenir and amulet, England, 1401–1700, Science Museum/ Wellcome Collection, CC BY

Figure 6.3 Zachariah's cross. A double cross, on one side Zacharias and his blessing, on the other St. Benedict and the lettering of the cross of St. Benedict, protection against the plague, Wellcome Collection, CC BY

Figure 6.4 Pendant reliquary with depiction of the Annunciation, Spanish seventeenth century, gold, enamel, rubies, crystal, pearl and rock crystal, The Metropolitan Museum of Art, New York

Figure 6.5 Reliquary, Spanish sixteenth century, Gold, rock crystal and enamel, The Metropolitan Museum of Art, New York

reliquary was small enough to be carried on the body or easily handled, suggesting it was part of personal practice. Eventually some pendants were designed in this style, which never held a relic but which were used similarly as part of devotional practice. The final reliquary, Fig. 6.5, is designed to look like a church altar, with enamel figures representing the crucifixion on the top.[6] It is only 5 cm tall. Underneath, within the reliquary, is a cross that is thought to contain a piece of wood that was part of the cross on which Christ died, and a container holding – it is said – a piece of the sponge held to Christ's mouth when he was on the cross. It was held by the Campana family before being purchased by a collector in the nineteenth century.

Relics

If more ordinary, but still wealthy, people could afford a small relic for their own personal devotions, more significant relics tended to be held by

Figure 6.6 Reliquary bust of Saint Barbara, workshop of Niclaus Gerhaert von Leyden North Netherlandish ca. 1465, walnut with paint and gilding, The Metropolitan Museum of Art, New York

churches or in the chapels of important people, like monarchs. Such relics might attract people on pilgrimage. They were often housed in significant pieces of jewellery or ornamental structures, like the pendant designed to offer protection but also to honour the relic they enclosed. Figure 6.6 is a reliquary bust, designed to look like Saint Barbara. She was one of four busts, along with Saints Margaret, Agnes and Catherine, that would have sat in the Benedictine Abbey Church of Saints Peter and Paul in Wissembourg and held relics in their breasts.[7] The relic she held is now lost. Figure 6.7 is an arm reliquary; it was a popular shape, designed to symbolise priestly authority.[8] They were typically placed at the altar and used in religious processions. This one holds the relics of Saint Fiacre, a seventh-century Irish monk who was especially associated with gardeners, herbalists and victims of haemorrhoids and venereal disease.

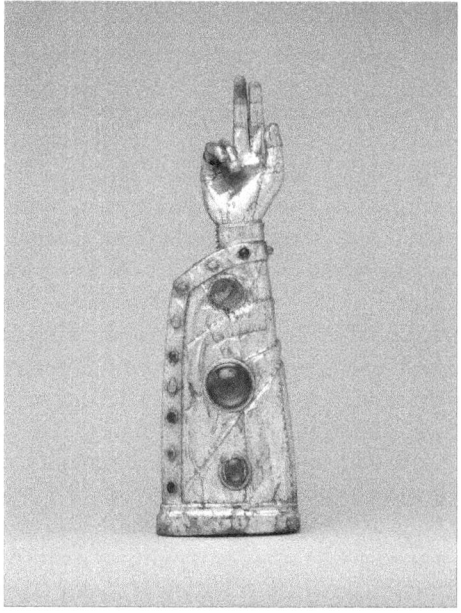

Figure 6.7 Arm reliquary, French thirteenth century with fifteenth century additions, The Metropolitan Museum of Art, New York

CONCLUSION

The personal devotional items – rosary beads, pilgrimage badge and so forth – are relatively small, held easily in the palm of the hand. Several of them have hoops suggesting they could be worn on a chain or string next to the body. They appear to be designed to be regularly used, touched and carried around. Each item is also designed to stimulate memory, whether that is through reminding people of the order of particular prayers or of a pilgrimage or particular spiritual story or event. Thus, we could imagine that they would be used in situations where people were engaged in spiritual practice, such as prayer, but we might also consider their talismanic functions. Pilgrimage badges and crosses designed to protect against the plague, and also worn on the body, could be touched when walking past a diseased man on the street, or when reminded of some portent event when in conversation. If prayer might be part of a routine religious ritual aimed at transforming the soul, and the soul was something experienced as feeling, superstitious gestures – the grasping of an item carried on the body – might similarly provide comfort and security to the Christian as they went about their life.

If small items aided Christians in their faith every day, the larger reliquaries, typically stored in churches or significant households, were likely accessed more rarely, perhaps when attending church or during particular festivals when a saint's relics were processioned and celebrated. Some relics, like the busts, were kept in place within the church and had to be visited on site, but the priest's hand was an item that could be carried by a group in a processional ritual, such as round a convent or through a city. Their location, as well as their uses, indicate that their function was not just to move the individual, but to help form a corporate Christian community. Worshipping together, an act that directed feeling towards God, should also extend affective connections outwards, reinforcing the Christian injunction to love your neighbour through group ritual practices. In doing so, such practices might have also produced feelings of loyalty to a particular spiritual or civic community, or even patriotism, when religious rituals were associated with the monarch or national politics. In such instances, the body was again important; faith was experienced by travelling to a particular site to visit a relic, or moving in a procession as a group. It required physical effort, that helped the body ready itself for worship, perhaps acting as an 'emotive'.

Using material objects and our knowledge of their uses offers historians access to particular 'situations' through which we can begin to consider how emotion might be mobilised, communicated and regulated. More challenging for the historian can be 'naming' a particular emotion. Rituals and activities may suggest people were 'moved' or were at least trying to enable an emotional transformation, but deciding what to call such an emotion can be more difficult. Was this love of God, loyalty towards a community, a sense of security or comfort? Historians might not have access to this information, and indeed such a need to name emotion might have the effect of forcing particular emotional experiences into a framework narrower than that experienced by the individual. As we have seen across this book, many people experienced an array of feelings at any one time, often moving across emotional registers during an interaction with others. Many communities allow such experiences to go unnamed, focusing not on what to call it but its effects. If the Christian was moved closer to God, or bound more tightly to their neighbour, then the purpose of an emotional performance was achieved. What word might best describe what was felt was less significant than what emotion can do to shape relationships and power dynamics, or enable historical change.

FURTHER READING

On Practice, Performance, Emotives

*Barclay, Katie. 'Performance/Performativity.' In *Early Modern Emotions: An Introduction*, ed. Susan Broomhall, 20–22. London: Routledge, 2016.

Barclay, Katie. 'Performing Emotion and Reading the Male Body in the Irish Court, c.1800–1845.' *Journal of Social History* 51, no. 2 (2017): 293–312.

Reddy, William. *The Navigation of Feeling: A Framework for the History of Emotions*. Cambridge: Cambridge University Press, 2001.

*Scheer, Monique. 'Are Emotions a Kind of Practice (and Is That What Makes Them Have a History)? A Bourdieuian Approach to Understanding Emotion.' *History & Theory* 51, no. 2 (2012): 190–220.

Material Cultural Practices of Religious Devotion

Bailey, Merridee, and Katie Barclay, eds. *Emotion, Ritual and Power in Europe, 1200–1920: Family, State and Church*. Basingstoke: Palgrave Macmillan, 2016.

Barclay, Katie. 'New Materialism and the New History of the Emotions.' *Emotions: History, Culture, Society* 1, no. 1 (2017): 161–83.

Barclay, Katie. 'The Emotional Lives of Wedding Certificates,' *Cultural and Social History* (online first 2019), https://doi.org/10.1080/14780038.2019.1589156

Corrigan, John. 'Religion and Emotions.' In *Doing Emotions History*, eds. Susan J. Matt and Peter N. Stearns, 143–62. Champaign: University of Illinois Press, 2014.

Dolan, Alice, and Sally Holloway. 'Emotional Textiles: An Introduction.' *Textile: The Journal of Cloth and Culture* 14, no. 2 (2016): 152–59.

Downes, Stephanie, Sally Holloway and Sarah Randles, eds. *Feeling Things: Objects Through History*. Oxford: Oxford University Press, 2018.

Eriksson, Ann-Catrine. 'Materiality, Rhetoric and Emotion in the Pietà: The Virgin Mary in Images of Piety in 15th-Century Sweden.' *Scandinavian Journal of History* 41, no. 3 (2016): 271–88.

Evangelisti, Silvia. 'Material Culture.' In *The Ashgate Research Companion to the Counter-Reformation*, eds. Alexandra Bamji, Geert H. Janssen and Mary Laven, 396–416. Farnham: Ashgate, 2013.

Hotchin, Julie. 'The Nun's Crown.' *Early Modern Women: An Interdisciplinary Journal* 4 (2009): 187–94.

Ibbett, Katherine. 'Being Moved: Louis XIV's Triumphant Tenderness and the Protestant Object.' *Exemplaria* 26, no. 1 (2014): 16–38.

Laven, Mary. 'Devotional Objects.' In *Early Modern Emotions: An Introduction*, ed. Susan Broomhall, 156–61. London: Routledge, 2017.

Nagy, Piroska. 'Sharing Charismatic Authority by Body and Emotions: The Marvellous Life of Lukardis von Oberweimar (c. 1262–1309).' In *Mulieres Religiosae: Shaping Female*

Spiritual Authority in the Medieval and Early Modern Periods, eds. Veerle Fraeters and Imke de Gier, 109–26. Turnhout: Brepols, 2014.

Randles, Sarah. 'Materiality.' In *Early Modern Emotions: An Introduction*, ed. Susan Broomhall, 17–19. London: Routledge, 2017.

Riis, Ole, and Linda Woodhead. *A Sociology of Religious Emotion*. Oxford: Oxford University Press, 2010.

Rubin, Miri. *Emotion and Devotion: The Meaning of Mary in Medieval Religious Cultures*. Budapest: Central European University Press, 2009.

Toivo, Raisa Maria. 'Religion and Emotion: Rosaries of Objects and the Associated Emotions in 17th-Century Finland.' *Scandinavian Journal of History* 41, no. 3 (2016): 289–305.

Walsham, Alexandra, 'Domesticating the Reformation: Material Culture, Memory, and Confessional Identity in Early Modern England.' *Renaissance Quarterly* 69 (2016): 566–616.

Williamson, Elizabeth. *The Materiality of Religion in Early Modern English Drama*. London and New York: Routledge, 2009.

Wilson, Ann. 'Kitsch, Enchantment and Power: The Bleeding Statues of Templemore in 1920.' In *Love Objects: Emotion, Design and Material Culture*, eds. Anna Moran and Sorcha O'Brien, 104–15. London: Bloomsbury, 2014.

7 Space and Place

Often when we think of space and place, we consider the physical environment where things happen – a room, church or even a field. Spatial theory, however, usually refers to a more technical definition of space as something that is 'socially constituted', not just referring to the 'material' world but also to culture and the meanings people attach to physical environment. Perhaps the most famous proponent of this model of space was the theorist Henry Lefebvre. Drawing on similar ideas to the performance theorists discussed in the previous chapter, he argued that space was not a particular physical environment but what was produced when we considered location (landscape, architecture, geographical place), alongside the human activities that happened in that environment and the words, discourses and ideas that attached to both place and people. Place is a particular type of space, given a name (Edinburgh, home) and which is especially associated with identity and belonging. This model for space can be applied to all sorts of situations – from physical places to online spaces to imaginary environments – but historians of emotion use it when they are particularly interested in including a discussion of the physical environment or human engagements that play out over distance in their interpretation of emotion. The use of spatial theory by emotions scholars has given rise to a number of related concepts, such as Ben Anderson's 'affective atmospheres' and the field of 'emotional geographies'. This chapter introduces these ideas, before exploring how they can be applied to historical sources. It does so using a discussion of emotions in empire, with a particular focus on the Jallianwala Bagh (or Amritsar) massacre, where British soldiers shot and killed a group of Punjabis in 1919.

SPACE AND PLACE

Just as performance theorists suggest that 'situations' are produced dynamically, in the moment, by the interaction between humans, their environment and the cultural ideas that inform these things, so do space theorists see space as something 'becoming' through action in particular contexts. This means that space, like the self and indeed emotion, is never a stable entity but something constantly being made by people. For Lefebvre, emotion and space were critically connected. Emotion is a resource that humans use to interpret their environment; they 'feel' in particular places and use that feeling to help assess meaning. These felt meanings, shaped by cultural ideals, physical environments and human bodies, become part of how a particular space was understood and so experienced.

Particular spaces also contained their own rhythms, a form of energy, that was produced by users but could be observed and 'felt' by those in the space. At times, this energy could build up, leading to riots or carnivals, or it could alienate people from their surroundings, dampening feeling and action. Much of the experience of space happened in the everyday, so that if people were felt and shaped by the emotions that infused their environments, they did not seek to question or transform them. Occasionally, in situations Lefebvre calls 'moments', people have a revelation about their environment that leads them to contest or transform it. These moments were conceptualised as 'felt' experiences, where emotion guided the human to an alternative way of thinking about or practising the world. Here we might think of Reddy's suggestion of emotional liberty as a driver of historical change.

An example of Lefebvrian space might be a busy urban centre, where people bustle by each other along narrow pavements, stopping for traffic at each street corner, waiting for a light to change, perhaps huddling under an umbrella as the rain sheets down and the light fades in the evening. One of the pedestrians is heading home after a day at work in the busy shopping district, hoping that she will make it to the train on time to get home at a reasonable hour. This might be a journey that she does every day, sometimes enjoying the energy and bustle that encourages you to walk a few steps quicker, to keep your eyes in front, and to manoeuvre around other anonymous inhabitants of the city. If it was much later in the evening, she might feel some trepidation, aware of the dangers that lurk in the night.

Largely she enjoys the bustle of the city; it provides a form of energy that maintains her speed and her willingness to tolerate the crowds, the stopping and starting at each corner, the often miserable weather. But on this occasion, stopped at a light, she notices a homeless man in a doorway and reflects on the injustice of poverty and the fine line that separates her from such a situation. This might be a thought, but it is also an emotional response, a connection, to another human, that shifts her from her normal interaction with the city to a sense of its alienating possibilities. Perhaps on this occasion, she just goes home anyway, but on another, increasingly noticing the ways that poverty is infringing on the city's environment, she feels compelled to demand a change, beginning a political protest to ask for a redistribution of wealth. Here a shift in emotional states is also one of transformation of political will and commitment, mediated not through meeting a charismatic leader or reading a persuasive pamphlet but through our everyday experiences. Space in this analogy is not just the city on which she walks, but her experience of walking, seeing, feeling and transforming through such actions.

A number of emotion scholars have developed these ideas. Ben Anderson has posited the concept of an 'affective atmosphere' trying to capture the experience of 'affect' as it is experienced within particular spaces. This is a similar idea to the emotions produced by the 'rhythms' of the city described by Lefebvre in that it recognises that particular spaces, through the way people use them and engage with each other, develop the ability to affect the emotions of those there. Anderson prefers the term 'affect' to address the ways that such feeling might not be consciously acknowledged, but experienced as a quicker pace of movement or an anxiety or tension that heightens the senses but is not immediately acknowledged. Affective atmosphere is also influenced by the sociologist Émile Durkheim's concept of 'collective effervescence', a form of emotional energy – often produced through group rituals – that heightens the sense of the group or collective and creates the feeling of being part of something larger than the self. Affective atmosphere is a concept therefore often used in relation to crowd behaviours, such as at concerts or during riots. However, like affect itself, many scholars dislike the concept, at least in its original formulation, for its focus on the 'unconscious' and 'prediscursive' experience. Others suggest that the idea of an emotional 'atmosphere' can be explained without resorting to the concept of affect; rather engagements between people and place can create a sense of atmosphere.

If Lefebvre provided a model of space as something performed, and where emotions help give it shape and meaning, and Ben Anderson explained how the emotional atmosphere of particular spaces moulded individuals within them, then emotional geographers explore the relationship between space, place and emotion across time and place. Some look at how emotion varies across place and why that might be the case – do all cities have the same fast-paced emotional energy, or are some slower and more sedate, and what does that mean for what people feel? Many are interested in how our surrounding environment shapes what we feel, looking at rural and urban differences, or how the experience of being in a church might differ from that of being in a nightclub. Building on findings from these questions, some then ask how emotional space shapes quality of life, happiness, health or access to political power. A scholarship of urban political protests and riots is important here, as events where collective feeling can transform space. Some, such as 'reclaim the nights' marches where women protested against the fear that restricts their movements, may even be designed to transform the emotional experience of a particular environment. This can also be the case in rural contexts, such as the women-only land collectives in the USA, Australia and New Zealand, that were, among other things, meant to provide land where women could live without fear of male violence or sexual exploitation.

There is also considerable work on migration and the movement of people, exploring how people become attached to place, how belonging is developed, and where it is not, and how definitions of boundaries and borders can be used to include and exclude, with related emotional effects. A history of refugees might highlight how anti-refugee discourse in a particular society might lead to feelings of exclusion and isolation by migrant groups, limiting their ability to find belonging in new communities and form connections with their neighbours. Here political discourses become an integral component of space, drawn on to produce meaning in a particular geographic context, and where both this idea and its reception are experienced as emotion by groups in that place.

The insights of emotional geographers, many of whom are also historians looking at past places, are useful for interpreting space as they help us to notice the many components of the human world – of the many 'resources' in particular environments that can be drawn on in the making of experience and how they vary across cultures. Perhaps more than performance theory, spatial theory, and the insights of emotional geographers, are useful for highlighting larger material and political structures, the things that humans have little ability to change at an individual level (such as the architecture of the city where they live or the political system of their country). Performance theory should account for these things in its model too, but as the theory was developed to help explain how people produce a sense of 'self' that is socially made, more emphasis tends to be placed on the 'resources' that humans have some capacity to control or shape than the larger material structures that they have to live within. A focus on space, with its stress on geographical location, architecture and the material world, refocuses our attention to our environment as well as the self.

The implication of this for models of emotion is that, if emotions are things we produce through performances, those performances are bounded by our material world and context. Our emotional experiences are not just restricted by whether we have access to particular emotion words or concepts in our language, but also by the tangible effects of things like architecture, environment, distribution of resources and so forth on our bodies. This can be seen particularly in the context of the British empire, where colonisation of land and people brought belonging and place to the foreground, requiring historians to consider how we might find emotion in accounts of our environment.

FINDING EMOTION IN SPACE AND PLACE

Like the performance model, historians seeking to use spatial theories should again imagine emotion as a 360 degree experience and give particular attention to where the emotion in question is taking place. If the emotion is happening in a building, then you might wish to think about how the architecture might be designed to enable or reduce certain emotions. Cathedrals were often designed with tall pillars or balustrades and light that enters towards the top of the building, features designed to draw the eye and so the face upwards towards heaven. Many nineteenth-century British courtrooms copied this effect, to enable a similar feeling of awe as a church and so to enforce the majesty of the law. Other spaces are designed for particular functions, but nonetheless produce emotions in those who use the buildings. The historian may wish to consider how the size of the space, its shape and the ways the design and layout encourage people to move or use it in particular ways might produce certain types of emotions. Large rooms with lots of light may feel brighter and so happier, than dark or poorly lit spaces, which may encourage us to be quiet and contained. Hallways where people can easily stop and make conversation may seem more relaxed or friendly than one-way systems where stopping slows down a queue of people; in the latter context, people may feel stressed or harassed, both if they walk slowly and feel a need to rush and if they are fast walkers stuck behind someone slow.

The material culture of a particular environment might also shape feeling. Some colour theorists suggest that particular colours and tones are more calming than others – like red – which are enlivening. This theory is often used in schools and hospitals that select shades of green and blue as being more suited to a calm environment. How people feel about colour however is quite culturally specific. Decoration too might influence how people behave, where opulent furnishings may make a stranger feel anxious that they might accidentally damage something, or reinforce the confidence of the owner and so enable them to exercise power over others. Furnishings can also be used as part of emotional displays, such as when someone throws a table in anger, or strategically places themselves behind a counter to feel safe from an aggressive customer.

If buildings and their fixtures might influence feeling, so too can the wider environment. As suggested above, an urban context might have a different rhythm from a rural one, so that visitors may choose to go to the countryside to 'relax' or slow down. For those who live rurally, such a stark division between urban and rural may disguise the complex meanings attached to particular places. Many rural locations are associated with stories and superstitions, from the 'fairy forts' that sensible people should avoid to the liminal site of the river-bank where danger or possibility are to be discovered, to the foreboding produced by a dark forest. When land and stories combine, inhabitants may experience quite different feelings towards particular sites than a stranger might imagine. A historian may wish to try and establish what stories or beliefs were associated with particular places. This might be especially the case for geographic areas associated with sacred rituals like Uluru in central Australia or tragedies like the Culloden Battlefield in Scotland, where the uses and emotional investment in a site produce distinct 'affective atmospheres' for visitors. Yet, as these latter examples also suggest, sometimes the stories attached to particular places are related to the material environment – the profound beauty of a geographic feature might explain why it became a sacred site for locals and is something that can also be recognised as important by visitors who are not from that culture.

If different locations help shape our experience of emotion, so too might the way we move through them. Are we speeding past on a train, or slowly walking over a long distance? Are we there as tourists, workers, migrants or refugees? All these experiences influence whether we feel safe, happy, tired or inspired by our environments. The novelty of being somewhere unfamiliar might produce emotional effects, whether that is curiosity, pleasure and excitement, or a profound disorientation and confusion when we fail to interpret a particular cultural code correctly. People 'out of place' may experience an environment quite differently from those for whom it is known and familiar. Moreover, new environments can cause people to reconsider themselves and their place in the world, movements of self that have affective impacts, and which are sometimes sought out by travellers. Here we might consider how the experience of an environment is a three-way interaction, between the cultural knowledges and experiences of the body, those attached to a particular site by the local community and the material conditions of the environment itself.

If landscape affects us, so too might our emotions impact on space. If space is something we produce in interaction with environment, then space is produced in distinct ways for each individual to reflect their culture, experience and emotion. Yet, our emotions might also leave traces behind, sticking to the buildings, landscape and objects that we encountered. This might be most obviously seen in situations where we physically change or alter the environment we encounter, acts that are almost always emotional by some definition. That we felt the need to make a change is suggestive of how environment becomes an affective process. We may also write or talk about our encounters with sites, and, perhaps if those stories become well known, such reflections may become part of the history of that site, affecting how other people relate to it. If we are very famous, our physical presence may even become associated with a place, creating new emotional attachments to that site that are informed by an encounter we had with it. Some places are also given meaning as part of our relationship to them. Home is a good example of this, a place which is associated, for most people, with safety, security, contentment but which is different for each family.

Historians seeking to explore emotions through spatial theory can deploy many of the methods we have discussed throughout this book, especially as we do not always need to consider 'space' as about a physical place. We could consider the 'space' of the letter, a site where people articulate their emotions at a distance from another and where both the written forms and the impacts of the postal system shape how that 'space' is produced in emotional terms. We can also deduce some information about 'space' through the material culture of goods or the information networks through which our written sources circulated. Yet, if we are especially interested in physical space, we might look to descriptions of places that attend to their appearance and construction and to the stories and meanings that attach to such sites. This might involve reading a broad array of written sources where places are described, from travel writings to novels to personal letters and diaries.

Some sites have also been drawn, sketched, painted and more recently photographed, and these can tell us something of both what they might have looked like and how they were imagined by people. Even a photograph is an artful form that hides as much as it includes. Maps too can be useful at helping us to imagine how a space operated, and for what they tell us about what the mapmaker considered to be important features of a specific location. In all these sources, we may wish to ask what was included, what was not (if we can figure that out) and so what mattered to those who wished to describe a site. Does a map only contain man-made features (buildings, railways) or natural topographies? Visiting a place can be helpful, especially at highlighting what went unspoken. Yet, we also need to consider how a place may have changed over the centuries; what has been added or taken away; how has weather, erosion or climate change impacted on natural features. Our own emotions may be deceptive as well as helpful.

If the physical environment mattered, so too does the geopolitics of place. The case study below considers an example from the British empire and that matters to how we understand what was going on. Whilst some situations may concern a local practice, where ideas of nation or empire were of less concern, often it mattered to people whether they were in a particular region or country, and where their location brought them into circles of political relationships with other nations. This is perhaps especially the case when we explore encounters between people from different places, whether that is tourists or colonisers, and for whom such geographic difference influenced how they responded to their new environment. Stories that attach to place and people then can sometimes be local and narrow, but at other times transnational or global, inflecting on how space and emotion are produced. Historians need to be careful to locate their emotional spaces within the larger histories that surround them.

EMOTIONS AND EMPIRE

Histories of emotional encounter between people from different countries, cultures and races are of increasing interest. Partly this is because it is in moments of cultural conflict and exchange that the unspoken and naturalised practices of everyday emotions come into the historical record. As so much of the ordinary – and much about emotion occurs in routine, daily practices – does not require explanation between those who are familiar with each other, historians often lose access to some types of emotional experience. But when meeting someone quite different, who lives in a different way and by different cultural rules, the things we take for granted can be highlighted and need explaining. This can make such encounters important sources for understanding cultures on both sides of an exchange.

Histories of cultural encounters can also be useful for giving us insight into groups that did not leave significant written records, or where such records were destroyed by colonisation or other disasters. European countries often deployed significant record-keeping practices as part of their colonising practices; records were how they managed people and ensured power. These records need to be used carefully – as they generally reflect the perspective of those who made them – but when read against the grain, we can start to develop an understanding of the people who they described and lived amongst. Over time, as different groups intermarried (or otherwise had relationships) and raised children, or where locals became parts of colonial bureaucracies, the differences between communities might reduce or evolve into new forms. Records of encounter are often useful for tracking such shifts and the new emotional communities that developed as a result.

If empires were enabled through love, they were built upon violent possession of people and property, which had significant impacts for how people
related to each other and for how such events are remembered today. British
colonisation of India was not different in that respect. Britain's early encounters with India were through trade networks, but becoming involved in local
politics, they quickly realised the opportunity for imperial expansion, using
their military forces to place local leaders who supported their interests in
charge of the various small states in the region. Over time, British power
became more entrenched. Direct British rule arrived in the mid-nineteenth
century, when a Governor-General was appointed to run the 'provinces of
India', drawing them together into a single national entity. This process was far
from painless, marked throughout by resistances, rebellions and wars with local
people, and enabled by the force of British troops. By the second half of the
nineteenth century, an Indian independence movement had developed, seeking to remove British rule. This was a complex and diverse political movement
that incorporated an array of charismatic political leaders, feminists, writers
and others seeking to remake modern India without Britain. It also included
regular 'rebellions', as the British referred to their acts of political resistance,
and violent reprisals. The Jallianwala Bagh massacre below occurred in this
context.

India was in many respects distinct from other colonised nations. Previous
to colonisation, India's various nations had rich written records and cultural
forms, including remarkable poetry and art, that survived colonisation. Many
states were relatively wealthy with important natural resources and complex
trade and marriage networks with their neighbours. British rule exploited
much of this existing infrastructure, integrating their people into these networks and power structures. One of the results of this is that historians of
India have surviving records for both before and after colonisation that allow
emotional practices to be compared and contrasted across time, and for the
impacts of colonisation on both Indian and British emotional communities to
be explored.

This historical context also created 'British India' as a particular emotional
space, one where the British and those who were in allegiance to them were in
an ongoing state of conflict with Indian nationalists, an expanding force. At
certain moments, especially when conflict became violent, this appeared to create a palpable 'affective atmosphere', a tension that heightened the significance
of particular local events and shaped the reactions of all involved. The rhythms
and energy of empire reflected that it was built on violence and conflict; the
love that mediated some of those connections seems to have reduced in significance as Indian nationalism grew in influence.

EMOTIONS IN SPACE AND PLACE

In 1919, amid growing nationalist activity by Indians across Punjab, and particularly in response to widespread public outcry over what would become known as the Jallianwala Bagh (or Amritsar) massacre, the Indian colonial government commissioned a report into how the police and military had managed political protests and disputes in 1919 and 1920.[1] The report is over three hundred pages long and is divided into 'majority' and 'minority' reports, the latter something produced by committees when they fundamentally disagree about a decision or interpretation. The report provides a detailed description of events around the Jallianwala Bagh massacre, with particular attention to physical space and several maps.

Consider the map (Map 7.1) and the descriptions of the physical space below. Can you develop a picture of the town and particularly the site of the massacre? What distinctive features do you notice? What is absent from these descriptions? How do these inclusions and exclusions signal what and who is significant to the report writers? How do you think the physical environment of the town and the massacre would have shaped the experience of emotions within it? How do you think this physical environment shaped the response to the massacre by observers after the event? Turning to a consideration of the space of empire, how did this wider colonial context shape events around the massacre? How did it influence the emotions of the various actors involved in the account? What do these descriptions suggest to us about British emotions – are they happy and content, powerful and secure, tense and anxious? How does this physical environment shape that? Give particular consideration to the Indian experience here. Can we read these records against the grain for their emotions and experience? Can we build a picture of Amritsar as 'Indian space', and is that significantly different from it as 'British space'? How do the emotions on display here attach to and shape the space of Amritsar? How do emotions shape the meaning of these events? How do they impact on the morality of the massacre as read by outsiders? What legacy do the emotions in play here have on how this event is remembered?

Disorders Inquiry Committee, 1919–1920 Report (Calcutta: Superintendent Government Printing, India, 1920).

Majority Report, pp. 27–45.

1. The first outbreak in the Punjab occurred at Amritsar on the 10th April 1919. Amritsar has a population of some 150,000; it is an important centre of the piece-goods trade; by reason of its position and of the Golden Temple, it is to

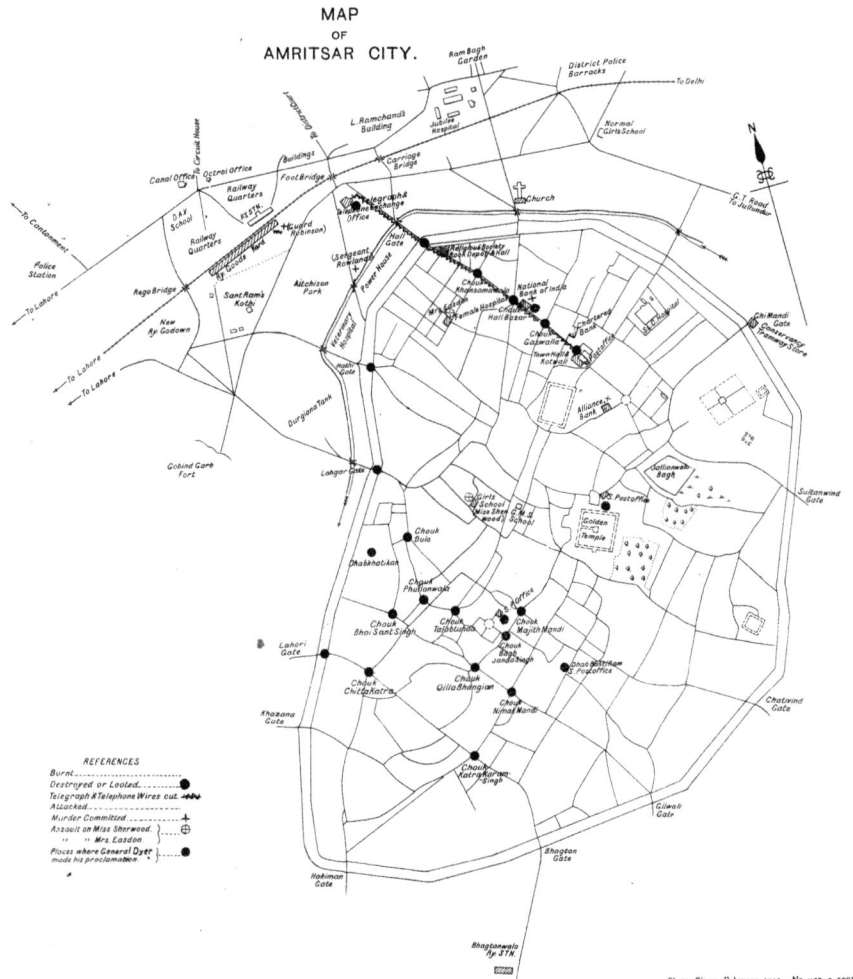

Map 7.1 Map of Amritsar City, *Disorders Inquiry Committee, 1919–1920 Report* (Calcutta: Superintendent Government Printing, India, 1920)

the Sikhs a city of unique interest and influence. The "civil lines" are divided from the city proper by the North Western Railway line.[2] From the Kotwali and Town Hall which are in the city the direct route to the civil lines leads along Hall Bazar through Hall Gate and across the railway by a bridge called Hall Bridge. On the left, as one crosses this bridge going to the civil lines there is also an iron foot-bridge over the railway. The railway station itself, with the goods yard and other offices, is on the further side of this foot-bridge. Apart from one officer and fifteen men of the Indian Defence Force the garrison at the time consisted of about 184 infantry (Somerset Light Infantry) and some forty to fifty mounted men of the 12th Ammunition Column, Royal Field Artillery. For such a garrison in any scheme of "internal defence" the holding of the railway line would be an important, if not the essential feature. Since the 5th April an Indian officer and 20 Indian ranks had been detailed as a guard at the railway station.

2. For some time before April 1919, public meetings about various questions, mostly but not entirely political, had shown that Amritsar had taken or was prepared to take great interest in public matters. [These public matters included several high-profile meetings, led by to two well-known Indian nationalist activists, Dr Saifuddin Kitchlew and Dr Satyapal, supporters of Ghandi. The government decided to arrest them, deport them from Amritsar, and intern them at Dharamsala, a different part of Punjab. The date of deportation was set for the 10th April].

7. The 9th April was the day of *Ram Naumi* – a Hindu festival on which cars are commonly drawn in procession accompanied by people raising cries in honour of Hindu deities. This practice was followed as usual in Amritsar, but contrary to previous practice, the festival was very largely participated in by Muhammadans, and along with the usual shouts political cries were freely raised "Mahatma Gandhi ki jai," "Hindu-Mussalman ki jai." The effect of the evidence before us is that the festival became a striking demonstration in furtherance of Hindu–Muhammadan unity – people of the different creeds drinking out of the same cups publicly and by way of a demonstration. To expect this form of unity to last beyond the day would doubtless be to expect too much: nor should it be condemned as wholly sinister or unreal because it did not last longer than mere demonstrations can. We think it clear that in Amritsar as elsewhere efforts towards "unity" had been made largely and indeed frankly in a political interest. That the disturbed state of political feeling in Amritsar would assist and did assist to throw the two warring creeds into a common camp *vis-à-vis* Government is intelligible enough. Dr. Kitchlew's influence in particular was, and had consistently been, in the

direction of unity and doubtless in Amritsar this fact accounts for more than does the general movement, which has for at least two years been well marked all over India. In these circumstances, while we regard the *Ram Naumi* festival in Amritsar as showing a state of considerable ferment, excitement and unrest, and as further proof of the influence of the local political leaders, we do not feel entitled to regard it as significant of special evil or to interpret the events which ensued after other causes had supervened by reading them in the light of a sinister construction of the facts of the 9th of April. It is certain that the day passed off without any hostility being offered to Europeans. The Deputy Commissioner himself got caught in the crowd and witnessed the procession from the verandah of the Allahabad Bank. He says "as a rule they were very civil, every car in the procession stopped in front of me and the band played "God save the King." A note of disloyalty which struck me was that a party of Muhammadan students dressed to represent the Turkish Army raised a rude demonstration by clapping their hands which is a sign of rudeness up here, that is all."

[News then arrived to the local authorities that Kitchlew and Satyapal were to be deported the next day on the 10th. They prepared by issuing orders that restricted movement along the path to the train station and around the station themselves. They also situated troops across the city to prepare for any protests.]

11. About 11.30 [on the 10th] however the news of the deportation was spreading: in the city: shops were being closed on all sides and crowds were collecting. A large crowd formed in Hall Bazaar and made its way through Hall Gate and over the Hall Bridge at the further side of which was a small picket of mounted troops. This crowd was excited and angry at the deportations and was undoubtedly making for the civil lines bent upon seeing the Deputy Commissioner. A Criminal Investigation Department Inspector who gave evidence before us and whom we believe, states that he was in the back portion of this crowd on the first slope of the road bridge and that members of the crowd near him as they were going over the bridge and before they had been fired upon or turned back, were crying out "where is the Deputy Commissioner? We will butcher him to pieces." Another witness, Dr. Muhammad Abdullah Fauq states that he was with this crowd and the cries were that they must see the Deputy Commissioner, ask him where these leaders were, and if he would not grant their release, insist on themselves also being taken to the same place. It is an ascertained fact that this angry crowd as it poured out of the city towards the bridge took no notice of Europeans whom it met on the way. Mr. Jarman, the Municipal Engineer,

passed it by and was not molested. There is on the evidence very slender ground for supposing that this crowd in its initial stages was possessed of, or by, any definite common intention save that of angry and obstreperous protest in force before the Deputy Commissioner at his house and for the purpose of overawing him. It was as events showed equal to anything but had not as yet resolved upon anything very definite. Violent and excited threats against the Deputy Commissioner we think there were, but it is not certain that these were many or that they were representative in the first phase of the disturbance. The mob had not armed themselves with sticks or *lathis*. Still it is abundantly clear that the crowd was not mere crowd of mourning and that to represent it as a large but peaceful body bent on respectful, or even lawful, protest before authority is a travesty of facts. We consider that the Deputy Commissioner was right, and had done no more than his duty, when he resolved to prevent entrance into the civil lines by any such crowd. Beyond this it remains undeniable of this particular crowd that it was likely to cause a disturbance of the public peace and that the public security was manifestly endangered by it.

[The soldiers attempted to clear the bridges of the crowds, leading to rioting in the town, property damage and the deaths of ten Indians and a European. Miss Sherwood, a British missionary and school teacher, was badly beaten in an incident that became high profile news. Reinforcements for the local troops arrived that night and martial law was imposed, including promulgations that people should not meet together in large groups. How well this order was publicised was a matter of debate.]

37. About 4 o'clock in the afternoon of 13th April, General Dyer received definite information that a meeting was being held at Jallianwala Bagh contrary to the terms of the proclamation issued by him that morning. He then proceeded through the city with a number of pickets which he left at pre-arranged places and a special force of 25 Gurkhas and 25 Baluchis armed with rifles, 40 Gurkhas armed only with kukris and 2 armoured cars. On arriving at Jallianwala Bagh he entered with this force by a narrow entrance which was not sufficiently wide to allow the cars to pass. They were accordingly left in the street outside.

The Jallianwala Bagh is not in any sense a garden as its name would suggest. It is a rectangular piece of unused ground covered to some extent by building material and debris. It is almost entirely surrounded by the walls of buildings. The entrances and exits to it are few and imperfect. It seems to be frequently used to accommodate large gatherings of people. At that end of the

Bagh by which General Dyer entered there is raised ground on each side of the entrance. A large crowd had gathered at the opposite end of the Bagh and were being addressed by a man on a raised platform about 100 yards from where General Dyer stationed his troops. According to the report sent by General Dyer to the Adjutant-General after the occurrence the crowd numbered about 6,000. It is probable that it was much more numerous and that from 10 to 20 thousand people were assembled.

38. As soon as General Dyer entered the Bagh he stationed 25 troops on one side of the higher ground at the entrance and 25 troops on the other side. Without giving the crowd any warning to disperse, which he considered unnecessary as they were in breach of his proclamation, he ordered his troops to fire and the firing was continued for about 10 minutes. There is no evidence as to the nature of the address to which the audience was listening. None of them were provided with fire-arms although some of them may have been carrying sticks. As soon as firing commenced the crowd began to disperse. In all 1,650 rounds were fired by the troops. The firing was individual and not volley firing. Many casualties occurred among the crowd. As General Dyer, when the firing, ceased, immediately marched his troops back to the Ram Bagh just outside the city there was no means at the time of forming a correct estimate of the number killed and wounded. At first it was thought that about 200 had been killed and this number was apparently referred to as the list of casualties. Recently an investigation into the numbers has been completed by the Government with the assistance of a list compiled by the Allahabad *Seva Samiti*. As a result of this investigation it was discovered that approximately 379 people were killed. Of these about 87 were strangers or villagers who had come into Amritsar from the neighbouring district. No figure was given for the wounded; but their number may be taken as probably three times as great as the number of killed.

After the firing at Jallianwala Bagh no serious outbreak occurred in Amritsar. Shops continued to be shut for some days but the life of the city gradually resumed a more normal aspect. In the immediate vicinity there was an attempted dacoity by the villagers of Ballarwal on that of Makhowal and one or two cases of wire-cutting, but otherwise there was nothing further calling for notice in this area.

Minority Report, pp. 189–93.
[Testimony of General Dyer]
Q. Supposing the passage was sufficient to allow the armoured cars to go in would you have opened fire with the machine-guns?

A. I think, probably, yes.

Q. In that case the casualties would have been very much higher?

A. Yes.

Q. And you did not open fire with the machine-guns simply by the accident of the armoured cars not being able to get in?

A. I have answered you. I have said if they had been there the probability is that I would have opened fire with them.

Q. With the machine-guns straight?

A. With the machine-guns.

Q. I gather generally from what you put in your report that your idea in taking this action was really to strike terror? That is what you say. It was no longer a question of dispersing the crowd but one of producing a sufficient moral effect.

A. If they disobeyed my orders it showed that there was complete defiance of law, that there was something much more serious behind it than I imagined, that therefore these were rebels, and I must not treat them with gloves on. They had come to fight if they defied me, and I was going to give them a lesson.

Q. I take it that your idea in taking that action was to strike terror?

A. Call it what you like. I was going to punish them. My idea from the military point of view was to make a wide impression.

Q. To strike terror not only in the city of Amritsar, but throughout the Punjab?

A. Yes, throughout the Punjab. I wanted to reduce their morale; the morale of the rebels.

Q. What reason had you to suppose that if you had ordered the assembly to leave the Bagh they would not have done so without the necessity of your firing, continued firing for a length of time?

A. Yes: I think it quite possible that I could have dispersed them, perhaps even without firing.

Q. Why did you not adopt that course?

A. I could disperse them for some time; then they would all come back and laugh at me, and I considered I would be making myself a fool.

[Testimony of Sir Michael O'Dwyer, Lieutenant Governor of Punjab, India from 1912–1919]

Q. I want to ask you a few questions about the Jallianwala Bagh incident. You say on page 10 "the casualties were large and regrettable but loss of life was inevitable when a truculent mob which had already committed murder and rebellion, assembled to defy authority."

A. You have got my addendum to that statement.

Q. Yes. I will deal with that. The view there seems to be as if the crowd that had assembled there had committed murder and rebellion. Is there any evidence that that particular crowd had committed any murder or rebellion?

A. I do not suppose it could be said with reference to any particular crowd, but Amritsar city, as a whole, had committed murder and rebellion.

Q. You treated the whole city to be in rebellion and therefore everybody in the city as taking part in that rebellion. That was your view?

A. The view I took there was that that meeting was held to show their hostility to Government and their sympathy with the people who had committed rebellion and murder.

Q. It may be that those who assembled there that evening may have been different people altogether from those who committed the actual murders and arson and other violent acts?

A. Yes, but they were there to show their sympathy with the people who committed murder and rebellion and their hostility to the Government which was repressing it.

Q. There is no evidence to show that they assembled there for that?

A. I think it may be inferred from the fact that they had assembled there knowing what the conditions in Amritsar had been for the previous three days and knowing that any such meeting had been prohibited.

Q. I am coming to the prohibition. But there is no evidence to show that the assembly there expressed their sympathy with those who had committed murder and arson?

A. I think the fact that they had assembled there was enough; they would not have assembled there without good reason, at a critical time like that.

Q. The mere fact that they had assembled justified the conclusion that they had assembled there for the purpose of expressing sympathy?

A. I think after what had happened in Amritsar for three days and taking that the prohibition issued that morning

Q. I am coming to the prohibition. You say they assembled to express sympathy. There is no evidence at all. You infer it?

A. Yes, I infer it.

CONCLUSION

The report of the Jallianwala Bagh massacre is notably focused on the British experience of Amritsar. The significant buildings marked on the map are generally those associated with British holdings – the railway station, bank, post office, hospitals – rather than local Indian businesses or homes; the Sikh temple is a notable exception. The map itself highlights incidents of Indian property destruction or violence, but not those where the British deployed violence in return. Jallianwala Bagh is marked on the map, but there is no symbol to direct the reader to the fact that a massacre occurred there. Similarly, the description of the town in the written report spends considerable time on British infra-structure, and considering how Britain would hold their part of the town in the event of a takeover, rather than Indian businesses or families. Throughout the report, British people are often named in person – they are individuals – but very few Indians are identified by name. Those named are figures of political significance or part of the British colonial regime. The rest are a nameless crowd, as are the Indian soldiers. That the British did not take information from the local population is particularly suggested by the fact that they could not account for the nature of the speech given at Jallianwala Bagh, despite their estimating 10,000 people in attendance of whom only 379 died. It is not difficult to iden-tify whose perspective, and whose property, mattered in this account. Even the minority account – which condemns General Dyer's decision – focuses its evidence on British testimonies. Thus we may reflect on the emotional invest-ments of the British in India, on where their concern and care lie, and on the defensive, self-protectiveness, of the report.

Despite this, we do see something of the Indian community, coming together both for a religious festival and later to protest the deportation of political leaders. They are described as angry, but much of their activity was non-violent, organised and orderly. The scenes of violence that occurred later were performed by a minority, and often followed aggressive behaviour by British soldiers, who wished to restrict the crowd from moving into the British part of the town where the railway station lay. Thus, we may suggest something of the 'political feeling' of this community, and also recognise how their forms of protest – organised processions – were shared with those used by the British at 'home'. Such activity can be refigured as legitimate political action if we read against the grain (an idea that the report writers themselves try to rubbish); the emotions associated with it may still be anger but of a form that is less 'unruly' and so 'uncivilised'. Rather we recognise the threat Indian unity offered to Britain and the capacity of local groups to enable the anxiety of their colon-iser through their political actions.

The British acknowledge that Amritsar is a diverse community; the 'unity' of some of its members is temporary and reflects the political will of the moment. But despite this, when reporting on Indian activities, they insist on considering them as one unit, an account that reinforces the difference – the line, both imag-ined and marked in their use of space – between Britons and Indians. The emphasis they place on this divide underpins the sense of anxiety that the British feel in this situation. They can no longer differentiate between political processions and violent action by a minority, because both represent to the British loss of control, something – at least for military leaders on the ground – that is felt as a direct insult to the person, a shame or humiliation that must be countered at any cost. Yet, anxiety causes its own problems for the British. For some, the reality of the threat of rebellion justifies this emotion and the violent over-reactions of soldiers on the ground; for others, it reflects an unmanly emotionality. It is not clear however that this amounts to an acknowledgement of the legitimacy of Indian protest and demand for the end to British rule. Anxiety might reflect the failings of the British, not the success of the subaltern.

Thinking of this account in terms of space, we can see how this insistence on British authority and the refusal of Indian identity within its production shapes the personal experience of Amritsar by people on the ground, or at least of the White British whose voices appear so clearly on the record. Their anxiety and its attendant violence are products of their need to control the space of Amritsar and the refusal of the local population to remain politically passive, something effectively impossible given their importance in producing the rhythms of the city itself. British military actions disrupt the flows of the everyday, closing shops and businesses, but normalcy returns through the trade and movements of the Indian population. Thus the anger – or whatever emotion best describes the Indian response to British rule – is the more significant in the shaping of Amritsar as the Indian population produces the baseline emotional energy of the city; their feeling determines the comfort of the ruler and the 'political feeling' of colonial urban space. That threat underpins all colonial relations in Amritsar, such that when the local population became too politically active, they needed to be 'terrorised' back into submission to quiet the fears of the coloniser and uphold their power, and where the physical environment of the city itself can be deployed to enable such emotional effects.

FURTHER READING

Space and Place

Anderson, Ben. 'Affective Atmospheres.' *Emotion, Space and Society* 2 (2009): 77–81.

Barclay, Katie. 'Space.' In *Early Modern Emotions: An Introduction*, ed. Susan Broomhall, 14–16. London: Routledge, 2017.

Blazek, Matej. 'Emotions as Practice: Anna Freud's Child Psychoanalysis and Thinking – Doing Children's Emotional Geographies.' *Emotion, Space and Society* 9 (2013): 24–32.

Brooke, Stephen. 'Space, Emotions and the Everyday: The Affective Ecology of 1980s London.' *Twentieth Century British History* 28, no. 1 (2017): 110–42.

Broomhall, Susan, ed. *Spaces for Feeling: Emotions and Sociabilities in Britain, 1650–1850*. London: Routledge, 2015.

Davidson, Joyce, and Christine Milligan. 'Embodying Emotions Sensing Space: introducing Emotional Geographies.' *Social & Cultural Geography* 5, no. 4 (2004): 523–32.

Lefebvre, Henri. *The Production of Space*, trans. Donald Nicholson-Smith. London: Wiley, 1991.

Marinelli, Maurizio, and Francesco Ricatti. 'Emotional Geographies of the Uncanny: Reinterpreting Italian Transnational Spaces.' *Cultural Studies Review* 19, no. 2 (2013): 5–18.

Morrison, Carey-Ann, Lynda Johnston and Robyn Longhurst. 'Critical Geographies of Love as Spatial, Relational and Political.' *Progress in Human Geography* 37, no. 4 (2012): 505–21.

Pernau, Margrit. 'Space and Emotion: Building to Feel.' *History Compass* 12, no. 7 (2014): 541–49.

Prestel, Joseph Ben. 'Hierarchies of Happiness: Railway Infrastructure and Suburban Subject Formation in Berlin and Cairo Around 1900.' *City* 19, no. 2 (2015): 322–31.

Robinson, Victoria, et al. "What I Used to Do ... On My Mother's Settee': Spatial and Emotional Aspects of Heterosexuality in England.' *Gender, Place & Culture* 11, no. 3 (2004): 417–35.

Soyer, François. 'The Public Baptism of Muslims in Early Modern Spain and Portugal: Forging Communal Identity Through Collective Emotional Display.' *Journal of Religious History* 39, no. 4 (2015): 506–23.

Soyer, François. 'Ritualised Public Performance, Emotional Narratives and the Enactment of Power: The Public Baptism of a Muslim in Eighteenth-Century Barcelona.' In *Emotion, Ritual and Power in Europe, 1200–1920: Family, State and Church*, eds. Merridee Bailey and Katie Barclay, 103–121. London: Palgrave Macmillan, 2017.

Indian Emotions

Haggis, Jane, and Margaret Allen. 'Imperial Emotions: Affective Communities of Mission in British Protestant Women's Missionary Publications, c1880–1920.' *Journal of Social History* 41, no. 3 (2008): 691–716.

Pernau, Margrit. 'Male Anger and Female Malice: Emotions in Indo-Muslim Advice Literature,' *History Compass* 10, no. 2 (2012): 119–28.

Pernau, Margrit. 'Introduction: Concepts of Emotion in Indian Languages.' *Contributions to the History of Concepts* 11, no. 1 (2016): 24–37.

Pernau, Margrit. 'Love and Compassion for the Community: Emotions and Practices Among North Indian Muslims, c.1870–1930.' *The Indian Economic and Social History Review* 54, no. 1 (2017): 21–42.

Pernau, Margrit, et al. *Civilising Emotions: Concepts in Nineteenth-Century Asia and Europe.* Oxford: Oxford University Press, 2015.

Prasad, Srirupa. *Cultural Politics of Hygiene in India, 1890–1940: Contagions of Feeling.* Basingstoke: Palgrave Macmillan, 2015.

Vallgårda, Karen A. A. 'Tying Children to God with Love: Danish Mission, Childhood and Emotions in Colonial South India.' *Journal of Religious History* 39, no. 4 (2015): 595–613.

8 Going Further

The history of emotions can be studied for its own sake, to better understand how emotions have been conceptualised and experienced in particular times and places, and also as a dynamic in a wide array of human engagements, and therefore an important inclusion to a wide range of historical topics. Over the last twenty years, this field of research has flourished and now informs debates in an array of historical fields and subdisciplines. This chapter introduces some areas of current research being conducted by historians of emotions that have not been tackled in earlier chapters, and seeks to explain the key questions and topics being discussed and why they matter either to the subfield or for historians of emotion more generally. Given the size of the field, this chapter cannot be comprehensive but acts as a starting point to some of the more established or burgeoning topics.

When conducting any sort of research, it is important to decide whom your research will be in conversation with, that is, which arguments and debates you are interested in contributing to and what scholarship you wish to 'advance' with your findings. The surveys below help indicate some of these debates and arguments to allow you to select areas of interest for further research. Each section is accompanied by some key reading; however these lists are not comprehensive and indicate a starting point only. Once you have decided the area of research you wish to engage in, you need to read widely on the topic to help you understand the context and how other historians are thinking about it. You then should identify the primary sources that will become the basis of your research and contribution to the field and decide which emotions theory best helps you interpret your sources and make your argument. Pulling all these parts – historiography, methodology and primary sources – together is what makes a good piece of historical research.

Which approach or method you should select is not always immediately apparent, but typically we want to use one that is appropriate to the types of questions that we wish to answer. If we are interested in political power, then Reddy's 'emotional regimes' might be especially pertinent. If we want to understand how emotion is used as part of everyday experience, we may use performance or practice theory. Sometimes we might combine different concepts, but this needs to be done thoughtfully as different approaches are not always compatible. Bringing them together requires a good understanding of the methods, how they are similar and different, and an explanation for the reader of why any incompatibilities do not undermine the analysis being made. This should not discourage you from trying it – theories and methods often only advance when people bring different ideas together. Similarly, you may find that the available theories and concepts do not really explain your data. Empirical research is often a good basis for developing new approaches and concepts to further our understanding of a topic. For all research, doing the wider reading is critical. Here you will not only get a picture of what we already know and understand, but how historians go about putting together their methods and sources to produce new historical knowledge.

MEDICINE, SCIENCE AND EMOTIONS

Today emotions are interpreted as a medical 'problem', whether one of neuroscience, biology or psychology. A disorder of emotion might then best be treated by a doctor or psychologist who can bring their medical training to your aid. Yet, emotions have not always been conceptualised through this lens, even if they have always had a strong relationship with the body. One branch of the history of emotions has been dedicated to exploring and explaining emotion through the various medical and scientific ideas and practices of different eras. They have suggested that emotion as a concept today has significant parallels with medieval ideas of the passions and affections, as well as considerable differences. They have charted how shifting ideas about the body over time and culture led emotions to be reconsidered, perhaps focusing on humours, nerves, or more recently hormones, tying them to the ideas of particular theorists or scientists. Such historians might also explore how these ideas led to the management or treatment of emotional disorders, from asylum care to medicines, to various therapeutic practices, to surgery.

Part of this history has been a focus on the emotions of medical practitioners and scientists themselves. This field of work was at least partly inspired by a stereotype that surgeons need to be dispassionate – to lack empathy for their patients – in order to do the job of cutting into people's bodies. Various historians have explored this question at different historical moments, noting the complexity of this claim especially when we consider all the emotions that might affect a doctor, not just sympathy for the patient, but ambition, pride, nervousness and so forth. If surgeons offered initial inspiration on this question, more recently historians have also become interested in the emotions of other medical personnel, including nurses and psychologists, and of course the experience of patients undergoing treatment. Histories of madness and insanity are also important to this discussion as an area with significant overlap with emotions scholarship, not least as madness and emotion both become the domain of psychologists and psychiatry.

Some historians of emotion are also interested in considering the relationship between the body and emotion across time, developing rich histories of organs, like the heart or liver, or of various body parts, like the hand. These are largely cultural histories that explore how such body parts are imagined, explained and related to metaphors of emotion. The heart might be the most obvious example as an organ that has been the location not only of love, but will, cognition, desire and many more human capacities over the centuries. These kinds of history highlight how certain organs can be associated with particular feelings, like sadness, or alternatively how they enable the body to be imagined as a feeling organism. One important discussion in this area has been around how the body is imagined in relation to emotion. What counts as an emotion? Pain is an important example here as something felt, but which has not always been interpreted as an emotional experience. Similarly, desire moves from emotion to biological function with the invention of the 'sex drive' by modern psychologists. Not all cultures think of sexual desire as a biological instinct however.

If there are a number of important works in this area, there remains a lot of work to be done. Much of the research has focused on Britain, France, Germany and the USA, and on the period from the late eighteenth century onwards. This leaves a lot of time and places to study. Even where work exists, there tends to be a focus on some of the more well-known names, figures or medical traditions. Histories of lesser figures, of medical practice in the margins or as everyday activities, and of how ordinary people understood their emotions in relation to the body and medicine are areas that need significantly more work. Cultural variation in medical beliefs about emotion has the potential to raise new questions and topics for study. There is also space for more consideration of medieval and early modern emotions through a medical lens, even if that is just to more clearly articulate how we imagine emotions and bodies without a scientific framework.

Key Reading

Alberti, Fay, ed. *Medicine, Emotion and Disease, 1700–1950*. Basingstoke: Palgrave Macmillan, 2006.

Barclay, Katie and Bronwyn Reddan. *The Feeling Heart in Medieval and Early Modern Europe: Meaning, Embodiment and Making*. Berlin: De Gruyter/ Medieval Imprint Press, 2019.

Boddice, Rob. *The Science of Sympathy: Morality, Evolution, and Victorian Civilization*. Urbana: University of Illinois Press, 2016.

Bourke, Joanna. *The Story of Pain: From Prayers to Painkillers*. Oxford: Oxford University Press, 2014.

Brown, Michael. 'Surgery, Identity and Embodied Emotion: John Bell, James Gregory and the Edinburgh "Medical War".' *History* 104, no. 359 (2019): 19–41.

Kaartinen, Marjo. *Breast Cancer in the Eighteenth Century*. London: Pickering & Chatto, 2014.

Macsotay, Tomas, Cornelis Van Der Haven and Karel Vanhaesebrouck, eds. *The Hurt(ful) Body: Performing and Beholding Pain, 1600–1800*. Manchester: Manchester University Press, 2017.

LEGAL EMOTIONS

That law, especially branches following in the English Common Law tradition, was dispassionate was considered a central value of the field. The twentieth-century Anglophone judiciary and legal system was vested in this idea, insisting that emotions – of judges, of lawyers, even of victims – should be put aside to enable justice. Emotion was particularly associated with 'bias' or 'irrationality' that could obscure judgement. As early critics interested in emotion and the law noted, this ideal was so significant to many lawyers and even legal historians that they refused to acknowledge emotion, including their own, when it was there. This could cause problems for the health and wellbeing of legal personnel and for the operation of justice. Legal theorists encouraged each other and legal practitioners to start thinking about the role of emotion in legal practice today; legal historians sought to find emotions in historic legal records, opening up a history both of legal emotions and of the concept of legal dispassion.

That an interest in legal emotions began with a concern about the emotions of judges and lawyers has meant that a considerable focus of research has been on the courtroom, and as a result on criminal law. There has now been quite a significant body of work on how different legal actors use and display emotions in courtrooms, whether that is weeping judges, the emotional speeches of defence lawyers and prosecutors, or the distress shown by witnesses on the stand. Courtrooms themselves have been analysed as spaces that shape the emotional experiences of those in the room, encouraging 'awe' of the law and the judiciary and promoting comradery between legal professions. In contrast, modern courtrooms in Britain can isolate defendants behind glass, far from the legal 'action'. That the practice of the law might be 'emotional' has been easier to both evidence and accept than that the law itself might be affective.

Yet, as new research highlights, the law is threaded with emotion. From legal defences to murder that use emotional definitions of 'provocation' to the emotions that imaginary ideal families are expected to feel in inheritance law, emotional norms and ideals have shaped how the law defines, interprets and evaluates human behaviour. Importantly, these emotions are not universal or natural but, because of the important role the law plays in shaping social values, can act as an emotional norm or conversely become outdated as emotional styles change. Historians have then sought to highlight how the law envisions emotion in particular historical periods and how these legal emotions impact on both legal practice and society. They have been able to chart how at certain moments the law provides more consideration of emotion than at others, and how changing emotional ideals lead to changes in the law itself.

An associated topic has been a consideration of emotional rhetoric and norms in legal records and process papers. These sources are significant to all sorts of scholars as one of the key types of evidence we have for ordinary people's lives in the past. Yet, legal historians have always emphasised that, as products of legal systems, their content should be read through a legal lens – this is not 'truth' but rhetoric designed to enable justice or to help win a particular suit. Yet, if that is the case, the emotional norms and expectations used by lawyers can tell us about wider social values. That expressions of anger were used to demonstrate a lack of manly character or that charitable love was prized as a virtue was not just legally significant in shaping the opinion of judges, but highlighted broader expectations around anger or love. Historians have been able to use these records to evidence how emotions are deployed for rhetorical purposes, but also what they tell us about emotional norms, styles and communities.

There is a growing body of research on legal emotion, but much of it has been focused on Anglophone contexts. Histories of emotions in other legal traditions are suggestive that more studies of cultural variety could offer important perspectives of the topic. This might especially be the case if we include histories of legal systems that operate very differently from European judicial systems, and instead work through oral cultures or customary traditions. More is also to be said on the emotions of legal process papers, rather than courtrooms, where only a few types of records have been examined in any depth, and on the different branches of legal practice, beyond the criminal courts. How emotions might work in corporate law and international law are both topics currently under study, and no doubt will raise new sorts of questions for these contexts.

Key Reading

Bailey, Merridee, and Kimberley-Joy Knight. 'Writing Histories of Law and Emotion.' *Journal of Legal History* 38, no. 2 (2017): 117–29.

Bandes, Susan, ed. *The Passions of Law.* London: New York University Press, 1999.

Barclay, Katie. *Men on Trial: Performing Emotion, Embodiment and Identity in Ireland 1800–1845.* Manchester: Manchester University Press, 2018.

Conway, Heather, and John Stannard, eds. *The Emotional Dynamics of Law and Legal Discourse.* London: Bloomsbury, 2016.

Milka, Amy, and David Lemmings. 'Narratives of Feeling and Majesty: Mediated Emotions in the Eighteenth-Century Criminal Courtroom.' *Journal of Legal History* 38, no.2 (2017): 155–78.

Temple, Kathryn. *Loving Justice: Legal Emotions in William Blackstone's England.* New York: NYU Press, 2019.

POLITICAL EMOTIONS

Legal emotions are a form of political emotion, given that the law plays an important role in shaping power relationships at all social levels. Political emotions can also be found in almost all social relationships, as power and emotion shape every part of life, whether that is relations in the family, between the sexes, in the workplace, or amid various social groups. This section however focuses on a narrowly defined 'political' to explore how emotions have been discussed in the contexts of states, nationalism, citizenship, revolution and political protest. If the law was, at least recently, imagined as passionless, the political has long been viewed as the domain of feeling.

Even before historians of emotions formally started applying their theories to politics, the scholarship of political life recognised the role of emotion within it. Histories of the nation have long recognised that where we locate our borders, who we include as part of the group and who we exclude have largely been questions of emotional investments and protection of personal and group interests. The nation itself is thought to arise from emotion, a sense of belonging and attachment to our neighbours, a political entity often underpinned by patriotism and nationalism, emotions designed to attach people to place. Thus a history of international relationships has been viewed as a history of persuading countries to put aside their own passion for their homeland to build connections with others. A scholarship on this topic has sought to highlight how particular ideas, values or symbols have been deployed to shape and produce

such national attachments, or to enable them to be put aside to aid coopera-
tion. More recently, using history of emotions methodologies, historians have
also highlighted how emotions are not just passive resources to manipulate, but
can be active in shaping what the nation is, how it imagines itself and relates to
others.

Political philosophers have also viewed emotion as critical, highlighting how
concepts of property, liberty, justice, democracy, common good and so forth
have been imagined as sites of emotional management and production. Much
of political philosophy, like legal theory, has focused on exploring how to enable
'positive' emotions, like love, trust, kindness, sociability, whilst restraining
negative passions, like anger, greed, lust, selfishness, for the benefit of the
wider group. The human, and its affections, has been a critical site of interroga-
tion and theorisation for those who wish to provide models for how people
should live in, for example, a democracy or a socialist state. Historians have
charted how these theories of the human and their sociable attachments have
shifted over time and in response to new ideas and historic conditions.

Emotions have also been critical to explaining political action, not only
motivating political protest but an essential dimension of what the crowd or
a riot consists of. Histories of political action have both tried to explain why
particular issues or causes became sites of emotional investment for individuals and groups, and how their emotions fed into and shaped the form of political action taken by these groups. Here emotion again is not a passive
consequence of historical circumstances or events, but a part of moral judgement and a dynamic in shaping how people navigate political life. If such a
history is suggestive of powerful emotions – of passionate investments that
enable people to act – apathy is also of increased interest to scholars, reflecting a sense that many modern people have become disassociated from political life, not least young people. But apathy is not unique to the modern period,
and these political emotions can be charted to particular historical contexts
and groups.

As an area of scholarship that has long been associated with emotion, new
histories of emotion have tended to provide more nuanced and sophisticated
theorising of political life, than new evidence that politics and emotions were
connected. Developing new insights through emotions methodologies however
is still relatively new, and there remains plenty of space for further insight and
application. Histories of individual political beliefs and feelings are also an area
where more work could be done; much research has tended to treat the nation
or political group in abstract, rather than thinking about its parts. This could be
particularly fruitful for helping us explore group dynamics, and when and
where an individual becomes part of a larger group or movement. Finally, a new

area of work that is developing is to consider the emotional politics of academic researchers, who are often drawn to particular topics by their own investments, not least a sense of injustice or desire to improve the world.

Key Reading

Ahmed, Sara. *The Cultural Politics of Emotion*. Edinburgh: Edinburgh University Press, 2004.

Eustace, Nicole. *Passion Is the Gale: Emotion, Power, and the Coming of the American Revolution*. Chapel Hill, NC: University of North Carolina Press, 2008.

Eustace, Nicole. *1812: War and the Passion of Patriotism*. University Park: University of Pennsylvania Press, 2015.

Fairclough, Mary. *The Romantic Crowd: Sympathy, Controversy and Print Culture*. Cambridge: Cambridge University Press, 2013.

Gook, Ben. *Divided Subjects, Invisible Borders: Re-unified Germany After 1989*. London and New York: Rowman & Littlefield International, 2015.

Gould, Deborah. *Moving Politics: Emotion and ACT UP's Fight Against AIDS*. Chicago: University of Chicago Press, 2009.

Hutchison, Emma. *Affective Communities in World Politics: Collective Emotions after Trauma*. Cambridge: Cambridge University Press, 2018.

Manning, Nathan, ed. *Political (Dis)Engagement: The Changing Nature of the 'Political'*. Bristol: Policy Press, 2017.

Nussbaum, Martha. *Political Emotions: Why Love Matters for Justice*. Cambridge: Harvard University Press, 2013.

HUMANITARIAN EMOTIONS

Humanitarianism does not consist of a single emotion, but if there is one prominently associated with the concept it is empathy. Empathy is the capacity to share or enter into another's emotional experience, and humanitarianism is often thought to arise because by sharing an emotion with the other we are inspired to help them. A much-critiqued history of humanitarianism, at least from a Western perspective, locates its origins in the eighteenth century and their prioritising of sympathetic exchange. The emotional education of the period enabled empathetic exchanges that were to transform political life, as Westerners channelled their emotions into 'saving' those who they thought in need of help. It is a narrative that ties empathy closely into a history of modernisation and global expansion, where Westerners encountered people very different from themselves. If such histories do not deny that medieval and early modern people experienced social emotions, such as compassion and charity, nonetheless modern empathy enabled a more outward-looking affective response to 'the other'.

If an early history lauded this sentimental rise of humanitarian feeling, scholarship since has sought to complicate what humanitarian emotions, even empathy itself, do in political terms. Humanitarian emotions have been acknowledged as consisting of more than just empathy, but the complex array of feeling that comes into play when making moral judgements. Power relationships have been critical here, as an imagining of empathy as something that should enable (positive) action from another also suggests that the other party has the power to act for the better. Thus humanitarian emotions often reify and reinforce traditional power hierarchies between those who have the power to help and those who must be rescued, and so demonstrate gratitude and subordinance. Scholars have also noted that, rather than the suffering is others motivating action, some people have taken pleasure in the voyeuristic sharing of their pain, feeling sad but taking no action, even leading to individuals seeking out such experiences for their own emotional benefit. Recently, as suffering has been actively deployed as an advertising strategy by charities or aid groups, 'compassion fatigue' has been identified, where people are overwhelmed with messages of suffering to the point that they no longer respond.

As humanitarian emotions are based upon an encounter with the suffering, a central concern in this research has been exploring what images and motifs have been effective in producing emotions in an audience. Here images of children have been noted as significant, where dead or badly hurt children tend to encourage a political response that is not offered to other groups, such as adolescent boys. Exploring why this happens and how different images are used across culture is a topic of interest. Histories of race and empire have also featured strongly in the scholarship of humanitarian emotion, as empire has provided a critical ground where 'civilised' colonisers have to balance their empathetic training with their exercise of power and their desire to possess the land, property and even the peoples of other nations. How groups that on the one hand lauded missionary activities, which at least in theory were meant to help the suffering, whilst also producing considerable pain themselves has been an area of much discussion.

A scholarship of humanitarian emotion is very current and evolving rapidly due to its relevance for our current media environment, as well as reflecting the current turn to transnational histories and histories of international exchange. Thus far however, much work has focused on Anglophone empires and media contexts. The relevance of humanitarianism within a broader range of cultures will provide an important perspective, especially given its association with imperialism. How other imperial states managed their feelings, and conversely how the colonised world empathised with their 'others', will enable a significant decentring of this Western viewpoint. Tying histories of humanitarianism into a wider scholarship on compassion, charity and similar social emotions has the potential to enable a refiguring of humanitarianism as something distinctly modern, whilst also broadening out what might be encompassed within the concept of humanitarian emotions. As much of the focus of the field has been on how representation of suffering triggers feelings, histories of personal intimacies and connections might also offer a useful counterpoint within this story, one that allows us to reflect on how humanitarian emotions are deployed in practice or reformed through personal encounters into something else.

Key Reading

Chouliaraki, Lilie. *The Ironic Spectator: Solidarity in the Age of Post-Humanitarianism*. Cambridge: Polity Press, 2013.

Hunt, Lynn. *Inventing Human Rights: A History*. New York: W. W. Norton, 2008.

Lydon, Jane. *Imperial Emotions: The Politics of Empathy Across the British Empire*. Cambridge: Cambridge University Press, 2019.

Warren, Mick. 'Fear, Empathy and Ambition: George Augustus Robinson's Friendly Mission.' *Emotions: History, Culture, Society* 3, no. 1 (2019): 72–93.

Wilson, Richard Ashby, and Richard D. Brown, eds. *Humanitarianism and Suffering: The Mobilization of Empathy*. Cambridge: Cambridge University Press, 2009.

MEDIA AND EMOTION

Humanitarian emotions are closely tied to histories of media, but the relationship between media and emotion can be considered in its own right. The word 'media' can refer to a wide range of materials, but here I focus on what we might traditionally call 'news' sources, like newspapers, pamphlets, social media and other mechanisms for exchanging information quickly between people or groups. A key issue for scholars of media and emotion is how the two affect each other. Can, and if so when, does media act on an audience to change their emotions and perhaps also direct their actions? When does a news story lead to political outrage and so revolution? Conversely, how do our emotions – or our desire to experience/avoid a particular emotion – shape our choice of media?

Examples here might be switching off the news to avoid feeling depressed or angry, or watching a horror movie to feel scared.

Historians of media and emotion, especially from the eighteenth century onwards, have been especially interested in tying a history of emotions to the development of the public sphere, that is, an area where ordinary people explore, discuss and seek to change political life. Early theorists argued for the importance of the news in the development of the public sphere, especially through creating an 'imagined community', a nation of people who understood themselves as part of the same group as each other. More recently, historians of emotions have asked whether this 'imagined community' was in fact an emotional community, and if that is the case what difference that made.

Building on this, others for different time periods have considered how the circulation of various media might create emotional communities, and even regimes, with impacts for how people understood themselves and their identities. Like for scholars of humanitarianism, a key topic here has been how various symbols or tropes, that is repeating stories, can be deployed for political effect. Moral panics have also been an important site of research, as easily traceable events where the media has been used to manipulate emotions towards particular groups, especially outsiders, sometimes leading to physical harm or political change.

Finally an important area of research is on the technology of media – whether that is early modern pamphlets or television and radio. How different forms of media enabled both the transmission of news and the production of emotional communities is an important question for research. Does it make a difference to your emotional experience whether you learn something through reading or watching it on television? Music has been of interest here, especially in the early modern period where ballads were an important form of news. Did music enable greater emotional impacts than reading alone? An important part of this discussion is the relative speed of modern media, where information can be transmitted very quickly and cheaply. The impacts of this are debatable however, as people can be overwhelmed with information, or reduced to expressing their feeling as button clicks rather than, say, a protest on the street. Moreover we might ask what 'emotional community' is produced when news is shared on a global scale.

The research on media and emotion could benefit from some greater reflection on which emotion is doing the 'work' of transforming people's feeling. Very often, emotional responses are identified loosely as 'emotional' or even just as responses to 'scandal' in a field that has largely focused on identifying the 'genre' of the media being explored. It may well be that emotional responses to key events will be complicated and mixed, but some more consideration of emotion itself, not just as an effect but as an active component, might begin to offer insight into the mechanisms through which media has emotional effects. In doing so, we might advance from the long-held belief in the power of rhetoric to persuade to the techniques, emotions and words that are used to get various effects from their audience. Conversely, if we know people seek out some types of emotional response through their choice of media, how that might impact on the persuasive effects of media could also be enlightening.

Key Reading

Barclay, Katie. 'Emotions, the Law and the Press in Britain: Seduction and Breach of Promise Suits, 1780–1830.' *Journal of Eighteenth-Century Studies* 39, no. 2 (2016): 267–84.

Fernandez, Luke, and Susan Matt. *Bored, Lonely, Angry, Stupid: Changing Feelings About Technology, from the Telegraph to Twitter*. Cambridge: Harvard University Press, 2019.

Lemmings, David, Heather Kerr and Robert Phiddian, eds. *Passions, Sympathy and Print Culture: Public Opinion and Emotional Authenticity in Eighteenth-Century Britain*. Basingstoke: Palgrave Macmillan, 2015.

Malin, Brenton. *Feeling Mediated: A History of Media Technology & Emotion in America*. New York: NYU Press, 2014.

McIlvenna, Una. 'The Power of Music: The Significance of Contrafactum in Execution Ballads.' *Past & Present* 229 (2015): 47–89.

Vis, F., and O. Goriunova, ed. *The Iconic Image on Social Media: A Rapid Research Response to the Death of Aylan Kurdi* (Visual Social Media Lab, December 2015).

Wahl-Jorgensen, Karin. *Emotions, Media and Politics*. Cambridge: Polity Press, 2019.

WITCHCRAFT AND EMOTION

The history of witchcraft and witchcraft prosecutions has long fascinated scholars for the seeming 'strangeness' of the events they describe. People whose claims to experiencing the supernatural were not just as a form of belief, but through active engagements with non-human creatures, have raised questions about the mental health and wellbeing of the communities in which witchcraft prosecutions were popular. Early histories often applied approaches from psychology to these groups, seeking to evidence the effects of group consumption of hallucinatory drugs, mental ill-health or mass trauma, following events like war or natural disaster. A more sophisticated body of work in the 1990s advanced the field by applying insights from psychoanalysis. Here the language of the supernatural became an opportunity to express concerns rooted in what could not be spoken – homosexuality or child sexual abuse – or troubling bodies, like the child or postmenopausal woman.

Given that the field was already concerned with the 'inner' person, approaches from the history of emotions seemed particularly apt for this field. Recent work focused on the witch has sought to understand how the individual witch used the language of witchcraft to articulate their emotions and subjectivities, where feelings towards the supernatural – such as taking the devil as a lover – could become significant moments of resistance to community norms, expressed as feeling. Here we might reflect on Reddy's 'emotional liberty', where the expression of feeling offers individual release within an emotional or political regime. Emotional regimes have also been noted for witches on trial, where emotional performances could not be 'unbridled' from their devilish reputation but where individuals also needed to display their remorse or innocence through their emotions. Witchcraft trials provide important evidence on the emotional life of communities and how clashes in emotional cultures or personal conflicts were manifested in witchcraft accusations. Gender has been particularly important here given the prominence of women and their excessive emotions in discussions of witchcraft. The emotions of witchcraft have also been widely represented within sources designed to shape public opinion on the topic, to produce a moral panic or to ridicule such beliefs. These include pamphlets, ballads, art and literature. As such, a history of witchcraft media and its emotional effects has been a topic of fruitful research.

If witchcraft has long been an emotional topic, deploying methods from the history of the emotions is a relatively new area of research. There have been calls for a greater historicisation of emotions in accounts of witchcraft and to take seriously people's experiences of the witch as 'real' (rather than standing for something else, like mental illness), perhaps responding to the ongoing influence of psychoanalytic approaches. As this suggests, research is still in its early stages at the present. New work on the supernatural more broadly, particularly ghosts, but also fairies, small gods and other unholy creatures, is also beginning to expand. A key advantage that the history of emotions adds to this field is its capacity to interrogate the abstract and unseen as both historical and meaningful.

Key Reading

Kounine, Laura. *Imagining the Witch: Emotions, Gender, and Selfhood in Early Modern Germany*. Oxford: Oxford University Press, 2018.

Kounine, Laura, and Michael Ostling, eds. *Emotions in the History of Witchcraft*. Basingstoke: Palgrave Macmillan, 2016.

Millar, Charlotte Rose. *Witchcraft, the Devil, and Emotions in Early Modern England*. London: Routledge, 2017.

Roper, Lyndal. *Oedipus and the Devil: Witchcraft. Sexuality and Religion in Early Modern Europe*. London: Routledge, 1994.

Spinks, Jennifer, and Charles Zika, eds. *Disaster, Death and the Emotions in the Shadow of the Apocalypse, 1400–1700*. Basingstoke: Palgrave Macmillan, 2016.

Zika, Charles. 'The Transformation of Sabbath Rituals by Jean Crépy and Laurent Bordelon: Redirecting Emotion through Ridicule.' In *Emotion, Ritual and Power in Europe, 1200–1920*, eds. Merridee L. Bailey and Katie Barclay, 261–84. Basingstoke: Palgrave Macmillan, 2017.

RELIGION AND EMOTION

The relationship between religion and emotion is subject to one of the largest literatures in the field of the history of emotions. Spiritual experiences, whether it was Catholic reflections on the passions or the neighbourly love of the 'hotter' sort of Protestant, have long been articulated as a form of management of emotion – the directing of human feeling towards God. There is significant research now that explores the understandings of emotion and emotional management strategies of a diverse range of religious sects, especially in a European context. These have highlighted the many mechanisms for directing emotion towards godly feeling, from worship with congregations, religious processions, the use of relics, paintings and other devices, abnegation of the body (such as through fasting or flagellation), personal prayer and private contemplation, diary-keeping and much more.

If some historians have been interested in how people get closer to God, others have been interested in how religious communities create borders and boundaries. Histories of religion and emotion have highlighted the considerable conflict caused by the Reformation and later splits within religious communities, and how that manifested in emotional terms. They have sought to highlight toleration as an emotional process, where tolerance is contrasted with a charitable hatred designed to reform the other. Histories of conflict between

Christians, Jews and Muslims are also significant, especially given the important role of emotional propaganda in reinforcing these boundaries and stirring hatred. Conversion can be important here as an opportunity to break down a boundary by moving an individual from one religious belief to another, something often described as a softening of hearts. Historians of emotion have highlighted how this critical religious process was imagined in terms of emotional transformation and the mechanisms through which this process was encouraged.

Theologies of emotion have also been a topic of research, as historians have sought to explain how many communities interpreted their emotional experiences as both embodied and spiritual actions. This is of importance not just to scholars of religion but to all historians as theology was often the central way ordinary people in the past understood and interpreted their bodies. In the same way that a knowledge of medical science helps us understand how our bodies work – and so how we experience our emotions – so too did theology provide a framework for interpreting embodied emotions. These histories have therefore wider implications for the field.

Histories of particular emotional–religious communities have flourished, not least those of monasteries and convents, sects like the Moravians, or various missions across the globe. In these small communities, people sought to apply their spiritual faith as an embodied emotional practice, with impacts on power dynamics for the group and wider society. Studying such groups has been particularly interesting for their insight into emotional norms when such communities clash with their surrounding neighbours or seek to convert those around them. This has opened up some insights into global emotions. Histories of emotion and religion outside of a European context are also being developed, not least as some emotions (like romantic love) are often framed in spiritual terms for many groups. Yet, this is an area where further work needs to be done to open up a diverse range of beliefs and their emotional practices. The emotions of secularism, and religion in secular times, are also ripe for further research.

Key Reading

Essary, Kirk. *Erasmus and Calvin on the Foolishness of God: Reason and Emotion in the Christian Philosophy*. Toronto: University of Toronto Press, 2017.

Haskell, Yasmin, and Raphaële Garrod, eds. *Changing Hearts: Performing Jesuit Emotions Between Europe, Asia and the Americas*. Leiden: Brill, 2019.

Karant-Nunn, Susan. *The Reformation of Feeling: Shaping the Religious Emotions in Early Modern Germany*. Oxford: Oxford University Press, 2010.

Mack, Phyllis. *Heart Religion in the British Enlightenment: Gender and Emotion in Early Methodism*. Cambridge: Cambridge University Press, 2008.

Walker, Claire. 'Governing Bodies, Family and Society: The Rhetoric of the Passions in the Sermons of Samuel Wesley.' *English Studies* 98, no. 7 (2017): 733–46.

URBAN EMOTIONS

How the experience of living in towns or cities shapes our emotion is a topic with some heritage – people have long thought there was a relationship between environment and our feelings – but one that has only recently been considered through the lens of the history of emotions. The urban, with its large populations, has for hundreds of years been considered a threat to both community and the individual by Europeans. The urban is anonymous, discouraging connection and leading to alienation. That people might feel overwhelmed or isolated when entering a new town was a topic of concern; that a more knowing population might take advantage of such individuals a considered threat. Yet if such moral warnings were perennial, in practice many people have successfully and happily lived in towns and cities since the medieval period, many preferring them to the 'dullness' of the country. Early histories of urban emotions have therefore begun to chart these anxieties, pleasures and experiences, seeking to ask how the urban affected different groups – men, women, children – as they use these spaces.

As noted in Chap. 7, space has been a critical analytical lens here, with historians seeking to recreate the feeling of urban space and to consider its impact in spatial terms. Place too is important, as a site of belonging. How people become attached to urban space, use it to form identities, and then later to shape their engagements with processes of urban renewal and the preservation of urban heritage have all been important. How the emotions of place have changed over time is a topic of recent interest, as scholars ask how meanings and emotions stick in place or dissipate at other historical moments. Migrations, wars, invasions, bombings and other events that significantly restructure cities and their makeup are recognised as important here, with new bodies and architectures transforming the emotions attached to particular sites. So too can local events attach meaning to urban space, such as the site of executions or a horrible crime and its emotional legacy for the landscape. As the latter suggests, the urban as a site for display and ritual is important. Processions around towns to beat the boundary or through town with music and banners can be used to claim space, mark territory and exclude others, all emotional experiences. Monarchs and other rulers have often used towns as manifestations of their power and feeling, with political displays designed to provide messages to urban inhabitants. In contrast, the rural can be a place of escape but also danger or loneliness.

For a topic long associated with emotion, the history of urban emotions is still relatively new. There is a huge amount of work to be done, not only on cities and how they vary from each other, but how smaller towns differ again. Whilst work is ongoing on cities across the globe, how ideas like the 'metropole' or 'provincial' shape the experience of particular places, and how that winds into emotional regimes, is still emerging. Histories of landscape and environment and how they impact the lived experience of the city may open new emotional insights too. We also need a history of the rural to complement these stories of an urban, a topic that is barely touched. If emotional geographers have given some accounts of being in place in the countryside and there is a growing field of environmental emotions, historical emotional experiences of the rural are still embryonic.

Key Reading

Barclay, Katie, ed. 'Section 5: Intimacy and Emotion.' In *The Routledge Handbook of Gender and the Urban Experience*, eds. Deborah Simonton et al. London: Routledge, 2017.

Kenny, Nicolas. *The Feel of the City: Experiences of Urban Transformation.* Toronto: University of Toronto Press, 2014.

Lecuppre-Desjardins, Elodie, and Anne-Laure Van Bruaene, eds. *Emotion in the Heart of the City (14th–16th Century)*. Turnhout: Brepols, 2005.

Prestel, Joseph. *Emotional Cities: Debates on Urban Change in Berlin and Cairo, 1860–1910.* Oxford: Oxford University Press, 2017.

Reyes-Cortez, Marcel. 'Extending Current Boundaries Between the Private, Domestic and Public Display of Mourning, Love and Visual Culture in Mexico City.' *Social History* 37, no. 2 (2012): 117–41.

GENDERING EMOTION

That men and women feel differently has been an important trope in many cultures. Following the widespread influence of the classical tradition, women have often been considered to be more emotional than men across much of the globe; the latter have generally been thought to have greater self-control over their emotions. Yet, if this was thought to be the case, who got to express emotion and when often belied such dictates, with anger much more often viewed as a male trait than a female one. All of this is a history of gendered stereotypes, rather than experience. One of the critical contributions of the history of emotion has been to offer these ideas up to scrutiny, denaturalising such assumptions and demonstrating the different gendered logics of societies around the globe.

Historical research in this area has sought to explore and uncover ideas about how men and women were meant to express emotion, in what context, and what form they took. Accounts of personal experience have been studied to see how men and women lived up to or resisted such stereotypes. One of the fruitful insights of these studies has been that, because a gendered logic of emotion offered multiple models for feeling, women and men were provided with alternative ways to express and experience their emotional lives. Stereotypes offered multiple ways to do emotion for many groups. Yet, if that was the case, the consequences of refusing to conform to emotional norms could be significant, not least leading to social exclusion, violence or shame. The interplay between the experience of emotion and the operation of power is highlighted in these studies, as individuals seek to live within gendered emotional regimes.

Research on this topic continues to expand as historians recognise the gendered implications of emotional practices in a wide range of places and contexts, and as scholars become interested in the personal navigation of emotional norms. Histories of masculinity and emotion are opening up but are still relatively new – men's emotions are often considered 'normal' or the 'default' against which women's are contrasted. But interrogating that assumption can be useful. Whilst there are some works on gendered emotions globally, a greater attention to gender and emotion in a variety of cultural contexts will also be promising, not just for highlighting diversity but at offering new emotional opportunities for men and women today. The operation of power remains critical to such studies, as does the intersections of gender with other identity markers, like class or race. Whether there are instances where emotion is not gendered is also a question that could be usefully explored.

Key Reading

Barclay, Katie. 'Love and Friendship between Lower Order Scottish Men: Or What the History of Emotions Has Brought to Early Modern Gender History.' In *Revisiting Gender in European History, 1400–1800*, eds. Elise Dermineur, Virginia Langum and Åsa Karlsson Sjögren, 121–44. London: Routledge, 2018.

Broomhall, Susan. *Gender and Emotions in Medieval and Early Modern Europe: Destroying Order, Structuring Disorder*. London and New York: Routledge, 2015.

Cancian, Sonia. 'The Language of Gender in Lover's Correspondence, 1946–1949.' *Gender & History* 24, no. 3 (2012): 755–65.

Steenbergh, Kristine. 'Emotions and Gender: the Case of Anger in Early Modern English Revenge Tragedies.' In *A History of Emotions, 1200–1800*, ed. Jonas Liliequist, 119–33. London, Pickering and Chatto, 2012.

Sturkenboom, Dorothée. 'Historicizing the Gender of Emotions: Changing Perceptions in Dutch Enlightenment Thought.' *Journal of Social History* 34, no. 1 (2000): 55–75.

FAMILIES AND EMOTION

The history of the emotions of family life is one of the oldest fields of emotions research, as families have long been understood as emotional sites. Some early work suggested that medieval and early modern Europeans did not love their family as strongly as today because patriarchal models and a high death rate made such emotional commitments challenging. In contrast, modern love was meant to offer greater freedom and autonomy for both husbands and wives. These ideas have been thoroughly critiqued by a generation of social historians who showed the rich emotional world of medieval and early modern peoples, and the ongoing impacts of patriarchy and gendered ideals in the modern world. A new scholarship on the history of emotions has sought to build on this foundation. One of the key developments in the field has been to historicise emotions that were often viewed as unchanging, like parental love or anger. New work has shown how parental love takes different forms and expressions in different places, and has highlighted both how anger has different meanings in particular contexts and how that played out within the life of the family.

The family is a key site for human life and organisation; for many societies, it was also a foundational unit of social order. Therefore the emotions expressed within families could be significant to the good ordering of society, to people's personal happiness and flourishing and for broader social power relationships. New histories of family life are therefore interested in how emotions impacted on family dynamics. How did the love of husband and wife compare with that between parent and child, or master and servant? How did these ideals and experience of emotion relate to status within the household, the ability to access resources (like food or education) and the capacity to exercise power or not? How did individuals who were excluded from power *feel* about that and find ways to resist or renegotiate their social role?

These questions have been particularly critical within a history of intimacy that has sought to better understand what difference living closely together with other people makes to personal feeling and wider power relationships. A particular focus of this work has been on the history of slavery and body servants, who not only cared for other people's bodies (dressing, washing, cleaning up shit), but were sometimes coerced into sexual relationships or raped. Here the possibilities of power opened up by certain intimate knowledges could be closed down by wider structural systems of racism or colonialism. Exploring how emotions, bodies and power played out in these contexts has been considered significant not just to individual families but to the operation of empires that relied on these personal relationships and the children they produced.

As this suggests, the emotions of the family-household could have widespread consequences. One of these is to recognise that the emotional logic of the household-family did not just stop at its boundaries. In locations where many workplaces and business were also in family homes, the emotional logics of the family could underpin economic decisions. A child sent to empire or another to inherit the estate could follow lines of love, not pragmatic emotional decision-making or even patriarchal lineage. People were willing to take risks for love. Many businesses ended when people died as they were not thought of as enterprises that existed beyond the family, but rather survived to enable family success. In this context, personal emotions and intimacies shape the economic relationships of nations and empires; family emotions mattered.

The history of family emotions remains quite focused on Europe and the Anglophone, with a few notable exceptions. Opening up a global history of family emotions has the potential to significantly diversify and complicate our knowledge in this area. Modern family emotions too are downplayed, somewhat surprisingly. While there are sociological works on the family and its emotion and a huge amount of psychology, work that historicises such feeling as a product of time and place is rather smaller, perhaps as such emotion often seems too natural to need explaining to people who have been taught to feel similarly. Charting histories of emotion as they are transmitted over time through families (lineages of emotion) looks to be an important area of potential work, as does the importance of family to memory and identity, something we can see in the emotional investments of contemporary genealogists and in the fashion for ancestry DNA testing.

Key Reading

Bailey, Joanne. *Parenting in England, 1760–1830: Emotion, Identity and Generation.* Oxford: Oxford University Press, 2012.

Barclay, Katie. 'The Emotions of Household Economics.' In *Routledge Companion to Emotions in Europe: 1100–1700*, ed. Susan Broomhall and Andrew Lynch, 185–99. London: Routledge, 2019.

Broomhall, Susan, ed. *Emotions in the Household, 1200–1900.* Basingstoke: Palgrave Macmillan, 2008.

Broomhall, Susan and Jacqueline van Gent. 'Corresponding Affections: Emotional Exchange Among Siblings in the Nassau Family.' *Journal of Family History* 34, no. 2 (2009): 143–65.

McEwan, Joanne. '"At My Mother's House": Community and Household Spaces in Early Eighteenth-Century Scottish Infanticide Narratives.' In *Spaces for Feeling: Emotions and Sociabilities in Britain, 1650–1850*, ed. Susan Broomhall, 12–34. London: Routledge, 2015.

YOUTHFUL EMOTION

The emotions of children are especially important to scholars of emotion (not just historians). If emotions are something we learn, then childhood is the time when they are taught. This has led to considerable analysis of baby emotions, as psychologists and other scholars have sought to explore if they can identify 'natural' or 'biological' responses that precede 'culture'. Historians of childhood and emotion suspect that such an enterprise is challenged both by the cultural training of the observer and by the emotional educations offered to babies from birth. There is even ongoing work analysing the doctors who historically conducted such research and their emotional assumptions. Most of the field however worries less about babies and more about how children were expected to learn emotions in a variety of historical contexts, highlighting the significant variation in strategies that different parents and educators have taken towards young people.

Such histories have sought to explore the emotional norms and rules taught to children, how they might different from those expected of adults, and when children should make the switch to adult emotions. These histories often look at educational treatises, advice books, school curriculums, reading material for children, as well as letters and diaries produced by children. Many historians have also sought to access childhood feeling, recognising this as a distinct moment in the life course and so where emotional experience may be quite different from at other points. Here the history of the body and child physical development can intersect with the history of emotions, both products of history and culture. Accessing the personal emotions of children can be more challenging as sources left by children, especially outside adult scrutiny (such as school), have only rarely survived.

Complementing the research on childhood learning have been some useful concepts developed by Karen Vallgårda, Kristine Alexander and Stephanie Olsen: emotional 'formations' and emotional 'frontiers'. Emotional formation describes the process by which children are enculturated in the emotional rules of their society; the small everyday educations that children learn by watching parents or siblings, of being corrected when making an error, or of learning from wider popular culture, and which add up to producing a person who follows particular emotional rules. An emotional frontier is used to describe the experience of encountering a different set of emotional rules or norms from the one you have been raised with and having to re-educate yourself to those norms. An example might be an Indian child taken to be educated by White missionaries. The frontier describes this moment of confrontation with new emotion rules and the process by which children (and adults) come to operate across multiple emotional cultures.

If much of the history of childhood and emotion explores how children feel or should feel, there is also a body of work that explores how adults felt about children. This grew out of a history on parental affection but has been expanded to consider how different groups and communities invest in their children, perhaps as symbols of future lineage or the nation. Such emotional investments can explain why representations of children are useful at shaping public opinion or creating feeling from entire communities. Like other emotions, however, the form they take is shaped by time and place.

The history of childhood and emotion is still relatively new, but from the beginning has been quite a diverse field, drawing in histories of an array of times and place. Critical to advances on this topic will be finding new sources that offer access to children's feelings and learning to read old sources in new ways. Much of the current work has focused on formal education or structured activities (like girl guides); more research needs to be done on children in family contexts and in unstructured play (such as on streets or in parks). There is also space for a more subtle reading of age that explores how emotions develop from infancy to young childhood to adolescence, and so forth, and especially how these are mediated by wider expectations for, say, work and leaving home. We need a history of how the child in the factory feels, of how new responsibilities and access to new environments shape their emotional formation or offer emotional frontiers to be overcome.

Key Reading

Barclay, Katie, Kim Reynolds with Ciara Rawnsley, eds. *Death, Emotion and Childhood in Premodern Europe*. Basingstoke: Palgrave Macmillan, 2016.

Frevert, Ute, Pascal Eitler, Stephanie Olsen, Uffa Jensen et al. *Learning How to Feel: Children's Literature and Emotional Socialization, 1870–1970*. Oxford: Oxford University Press, 2014.

Jarzebowski, Claudia, and Thomas Max Safley, eds. *Childhood and Emotion: Across Cultures 1450–1800*. Abingdon: Routledge, 2014.

Marshall, Sherrin. '"Dutiful Love and Natural Affection": Parent-Child Relationships in the Early Modern Netherlands.' In *Early Modern Europe: Issues and Interpretation*, eds. James B. Collins and Karen L. Taylor, 138–52. Oxford: Blackwell, 2006.

Olsen, Stephanie, ed. *Childhood, Youth and Emotions in Modern History: National, Colonial and Global Perspectives*. Basingstoke: Palgrave Macmillan, 2015.

Olsen, Stephanie. 'The History of Childhood and the Emotional Turn.' *History Compass* 15, no. 11 (2017): 1–10.

Stearns, Peter. 'Obedience and Emotion: a Challenge in the Emotional History of Childhood.' *Journal of Social History* 47, no. 3 (2014): 593–611.

CONCLUSION

Approaches from the history of emotions can be applied to many topics, and those suggested here are not comprehensive. A key consideration might be to reflect on whether something you are studying satisfactorily explains a phenomenon; perhaps it just assumes a connection between two things (like watching the news and political protest) without explaining how you get from a to b. Often emotions are useful as they explain how people make decisions or are transformed from one state to another, from calm to angry. Analysing the emotion work that happened in that context not only helps you explain what happened but can also open up new relationships of power or new questions to be answered. You might also think that emotions work needs to be done if a topic contains lots of emotion words, but nobody stops to consider what they mean in that historical context, perhaps assuming that they are the same as today. Asking why those emotions are there and what they mean for that society can open up new approaches to a topic.

This book has placed emphasis on the various concepts and methodologies that historians have used to help them better analyse their source material and to understand how emotions operate. They can be useful for this and for explaining your thinking to your reader when you make assumptions about how emotions work. Yet one of the key things that these concepts demonstrate is that historians, each in their own way, are grappling with a similar set of questions about emotions, bodies, language and cultural variation, and seeking ways to address them. It may be that your research indicates more productive approaches than what is offered here. Or you may feel that more traditional historical methodologies allow you to come to similar conclusions in your research. As you may notice above, many of the debates happening in the history of emotions are not concerned directly with these issues of method but how we might more satisfactorily understand specific cultural ideas or experiences of emotion. When the history of emotions engages with other historical debates and questions, sometimes the central concern of the research shifts too, no longer trying to explore what emotion is but how it helps us better understand a different problem. In this way, the history of emotions has the potential to be used in a much wider range of histories than at present.

Further Reading and Resources

The history of emotions is a burgeoning field, and new publications and resources are being developed regularly. Below is a range of websites, resources and scholarship that offers wider information on the field. Sources that appear in other chapters are not repeated here, so use along with the rest of the book.

BLOGS AND WEBSITES

Blogs often provide short, non-academic introductions to topics in the history of emotions, and access to cutting-edge scholarship before it is published by a scholarly outlet. There are also three major emotions centres – the ARC Centre of Excellence in the History of Emotions, Australia; the Queen Mary, University of London Centre for the History of Emotions, and the Max Planck Centre for the History of Emotions, Berlin. Their websites often contain useful resources for students and researchers. Notably the ARC Centre has a number of resources for school teachers, as well as for researchers, including a large bibliography of emotions scholarship.

ARC Centre for the History of Emotions Blog, https://historiesofemotion.com/

QMUL Centre for the History of Emotions Blog, https://emotionsblog.history.qmul.ac.uk/

Emotional Objects: Touching Emotions in History, https://emotionalobjects.wordpress.com/

Objects and Emotions Blog, www.objectsandemotions.org/blog

Embodied Emotions, http://embodiedemotions.com/

Max Planck History of Emotions, www.history-of-emotions.mpg.de/en

Bibliography of History of Emotions, www.zotero.org/groups/che_bibliography_history_of_emotions/items

PODCASTS AND VIDEOS

Podcasts and videos allow you to listen to research on the history of emotions on the go. These can include recordings of scholarly presentations and talks, but also podcasts designed for more leisurely listening.

ARC Centre for the History of Emotions Vimeo, https://vimeo.com/thinkemotions

ARC Centre for the History of Emotions Podcasts, https://soundcloud.com/emotions_make_history

QMUL Centre for the History of Emotions Podcasts, https://soundcloud.com/user-357683788

JOURNALS

There are now a number of academic journals that are dedicated to publishing research in the history and sociology of the emotions. Check in regularly with these publications to access the latest research, and think of them when you are ready to publish too.

Emotion Review

Emotions and Society

Emotions: History, Culture, Society

Emotion, Space and Society

FURTHER READING

Each chapter has included reading to take you further on a topic. You may have noticed that sometimes historians of emotion have to combine their emotions research with wider reading that is not directly related to emotions. This is because the history of emotions is a new topic in some areas. However, by combining wider research on the historical topic you are interested in with methodologies from the history of emotions, you can start to see how emotions can be important to a wide range of subjects. Below is some current research from historians and similar scholars who have been thinking about emotion. It is divided into some general introductory texts that give overviews of the field, and specialist topics that give a sense of the breadth of current scholarship.

General Introductions

Biess, Frank, et al. 'History of Emotions.' *German History* 28, no.1 (2010): 67–80.

Brooks, Ann. *Genealogies of Emotions, Intimacies, Desires*. New York: Routledge, 2017.

Broomhall, Susan, Jane W. Davidson and Andrew Lynch, eds. *A Cultural History of Emotions, 6 vols*. London: Bloomsbury, 2019.

Champion, Michael, and Juanita Feros Reyes, eds. *Understanding Emotions in Early Europe*. Turnhout: Brepols, 2015.

Dixon, Thomas. *From Passions to Emotions: The Creation of a Secular Psychological Category*. Cambridge: Cambridge University Press, 2003.

Frevert, Ute. *Emotions in History: Lost and Found*. New York: Central European Press, 2011.

Matt, Susan J. 'Current Emotion Research in History: Or, Doing History from the Inside Out.' *Emotion Review* 3, no. 1 (2011): 117–24.

Paster, Gail Kern, Katherine Rowe and Mary Floyd-Wilson, eds. *Reading the Early Modern Passions: Essays in the Cultural History of Emotions*. Philadelphia: Pennsylvania University Press, 2004.

Plamper, Jan. *The History of Emotions: An Introduction*. Oxford: Oxford University Press, 2015.

Seymour, Mark. 'Emotional Arenas: From Provincial Circus to National Courtroom in Late Nineteenth-Century Italy.' *Rethinking History* 16, no. 2 (2012): 177–97.

Stearns, Peter N. 'History of Emotions: Issues of Change and Impact.' In *The Handbook of Emotions*, eds. Michael Lewis, Jeanette M. Haviland-Jones and Lisa Feldman-Barrett, 17–31. New York: Guilford Press, 2010.

Stearns, Carol Z. and Peter N. Stearns, eds. *Emotion and Social Change: Toward a New Psychohistory*. New York: Holmes and Meier, 1988.

Trigg, Stephanie. 'Introduction: Emotional Histories – Beyond the Personalization of the Past and the Abstraction of Affect Theory.' *Exemplaria* 26, no. 1 (2014): 3–15.

Specialist Reading

Åhäl, Linda, and Thomas Gregory. *Emotions, Politics and War*. New York: Routledge, 2015.

Alberti, Fay Bound. *Matters of the Heart: History, Medicine and Emotion.* Oxford: Oxford University Press, 2010.

Alberti, Fay Bound. *A Biography of Loneliness.* Oxford: Oxford University Press, 2019.

Amler, Mark. *Affective Literacies: Writing and Multilingualism in the Late Middle Ages.* Turnhout: Brepols, 2011.

Anderson, E. N. *Ecologies of the Heart: Emotion, Belief, and the Environment.* Oxford: Oxford University Press, 1996.

Arellano, Jerónimo. *Magical Realism and the History of the Emotions in Latin America.* Lanham: Bucknell University Press, 2015.

Auerbach, Jeffrey A. *Imperial Boredom: Monotony and the British Empire.* Oxford: Oxford University Press, 2018.

Barbalet, Jack M. *Emotion, Social Theory, and Social Structure: A Macrosociological Approach.* Cambridge: Cambridge University Press, 2001.

Barbalet, Jack M. *Emotions and Sociology.* Oxford: Blackwell, 2002.

Barclay, Katie. 'Sounds of Sedition: Music and Emotion in Ireland, 1780–1845.' *Cultural History* 3, no. 1 (2014): 54–80.

Barclay, Katie. 'Narrative, Law and Emotion: Husband Killers in Early Nineteenth-Century Ireland.' *Journal of Legal History* 38, no. 2 (2017): 203–27.

Barclay, Katie, 'Love and Violence in the Music of Late Modernity.' *Popular Music and Society* 41, no. 5 (2018): 539–55.

Barclay, Katie. 'Natural Affection, the Patriarchal Family and the "Strict Settlement" Debate: A Response from the History of Emotions.' *Eighteenth Century: Theory and Interpretation* 58, no. 3 (2018): 309–20.

Barclay, Katie. 'Loving the Illegitimate Child in Eighteenth-Century Scotland.' *Transactions of the Royal Historical Society* 29 (2019): 105–25.

Barclay, Katie. 'Falling in Love with the Dead.' *Rethinking History* 22, no. 4 (2019): 459–73.

Barclay, Katie. 'Love and Other Emotions.' In *The Routledge History of Women in Early Modern Europe*, ed. Amanda Capern, 77–96. London: Routledge, 2020.

Barclay, Katie, and Rosalind Carr. 'Women, Love and Power in Enlightenment Scotland.' *Women's History Review* 27, no. 2 (2018): 176–98.

Barclay, Katie, Jeffrey Meek and Andrea Thomson, eds. *Courtship, Marriage and Marriage Breakdown: Approaches from the History of Emotion.* London: Routledge, 2020.

Bergman Blix, Stina, and Åsa Wettergren. 'A Sociological Perspective on Emotions in the Judiciary.' *Emotion Review* 23 (2015): 1–6.

Berlant, Lauren. *Compassion: The Culture and Politics of an Emotion*. Hove: Psychology Press, 2004.

Berlant, Lauren. *Cruel Optimism*. Durham: Duke University Press, 2011.

Biess, Frank. '"Everybody Has a Chance": Nuclear Angst, Civil Defence, and the History of Emotions in Postwar West Germany.' *German History* 27, no. 2 (2009): 215–43.

Biess, Frank, and Daniel Gross, eds. *Science and Emotions After 1945: A Transatlantic Perspective*. Chicago: Chicago University Press, 2014.

Bladow, Kyle, and Jennifer Ladino, eds. *Affective Ecocriticism: Emotion, Embodiment, Environment*. Lincoln: University of Nebraska Press, 2018.

Bleiker, Roland, ed. *Visual Global Politics*. New York: Routledge, 2018.

Blick, Sarah. *Push Me, Pull You: Imaginative, Emotional, Physical, and Spatial Interaction in Late Medieval and Renaissance Art*. Leiden: Brill, 2011.

Boddice, Rob, ed. *Pain and Emotion in Modern History*. Basingstoke: Palgrave Macmillan, 2014.

Boddice, Rob. *Pain: A Very Short Introduction*. Oxford: Oxford University Press, 2017.

Boltanski, Luc. *Distant Suffering: Morality, Media and Politics*. Cambridge: Cambridge University Press, 1999.

Borges, Marcelo J., and Sonia Cancian, eds. *Migrant Letters: Emotional Language, Mobile Identities, and Writing Practices in Historical Perspective*. London: Routledge, 2018.

Bourke, Joanna. *Fear: A Cultural History*. London: Hachette, 2005.

Braddick, Michael, and Joanna Innes, eds. *Suffering and Happiness in England, 1550–1850: Narratives and Representations*. Oxford: Oxford University Press, 2017.

Brandsma, Frank, Carolyne Larrington and Corinne Saunders, eds. *Emotions in Medieval Arthurian Literature: Body, Mind, Voice*. Woodbridge: Boydell and Brewer, 2015.

Bristow, Tom. *The Anthropocene Lyric: An Affective Geography of Poetry, Person, Place*. Basingstoke: Palgrave Macmillan, 2015.

Broomhall, Susan. *Authority, Gender and Emotions in Late Medieval and Early Modern England*. Basingstoke: Palgrave Macmillan, 2015.

Brown, Michael. 'Surgery and Emotion: The Era Before Anaesthesia.' In *The Palgrave Handbook of the History of Surgery*, ed. Thomas Schlich, 327–48. Basingstoke: Palgrave Macmillan, 2018.

Cancian, Francesca M. 'The Feminization of Love.' *Signs* 11, no. 4 (1986): 692–709.

Cancian, Francesca M., and Steven Gordon. 'Changing Emotion Norms in Marriage: Love and Anger in US Women's Magazines Since 1900.' *Gender and Society* 2, no. 3 (1988): 308–42.

Caneque, Alejandro. 'The Emotions of Power: Love, Anger and Fear, or How to Rule the Spanish Empire.' In *Emotions and Daily Life in Colonial Mexico*, eds. Javier Villa-Flores and Sonya Lipsett-Rivera, 89–121. Albuquerque: University of New Mexico Press, 2014.

Carrera, Elena, ed. *Emotions and Health, 1200–1700*. Leiden: Brill, 2013.

Chatterjee, Elizabeth, Sneha Krishnan and Megan Eaton Robb. 'Feeling Modern: The History of Emotions in Urban South Asia.' *JRAS* 27, no. 4 (2017): 539–57.

Coleborne, Catherine. 'Families, Patients and Emotions: Asylums for the Insane in Colonial Australia and New Zealand, c. 1880–1910.' *Social History of Medicine* 19, no. 3 (2006): 425–42.

Connolly, Thomas. *Mourning into Joy: Music, Raphael, and Saint Cecilia*. New Haven: Yale University Press, 1995.

Costigliola, Frank. '"Unceasing Pressure for Penetration": Gender, Pathology, and Emotion in George Kennan's Formation of the Cold War.' *Journal of American History* 83, no. 4 (1997): 1309–39.

Costigliola, Frank. '"I Had Come as a Friend": Emotion, Culture, and Ambiguity in the Formation of the Cold War, 1943–45.' *Cold War History* 1, no. 1 (2000): 103–28.

Crozier-De Rosa, Sharon. *Shame and the Anti-feminist Backlash: Britain, Ireland and Australia, 1890–1920*. London: Routledge, 2018.

D'Arcens, Louise. *Comic Medievalism: Laughing at the Middle Ages*. New York: D. S. Brewer, 2014.

Davidson, Jane W., and Sandra Garrido, eds. *Music and Mourning*. Abingdon: Routledge, 2016.

Dell, Helen, and Helen Hickey, eds. *Singing Death: Reflections on Music and Mortality*. London: Routledge, 2017.

Dickey, Stephanie, and Herman Roodenburg, eds. *Passion in the Arts of the Early Modern Netherlands*. Leiden: Brill, 2010.

Downes, Stephanie, Andrew Lynch and Katrina O'Loughlin, eds. *Emotions and War: Medieval to Romantic Literature*. Basingstoke: Palgrave, 2015.

Essary, Kirk, Juanita Ruys and Michael Champion, eds. *Before Emotion: The Language of Feeling, 400–1800*. London: Routledge, 2019.

Febvre, Lucien. 'Sensibility and History: How to Reconstitute the Emotional Life of the Past,' trans. K. Folca. In *A New Kind of History: From the Writings of Febvre*, ed. Peter Burke, 12–26. New York: Harper & Row, 1973.

Francis, Martin. 'Tears, Tantrums, and Bared Teeth: The Emotional Economy of Three Conservative Prime Ministers, 1951–1963.' *Journal of British Studies* 41, no. 3 (2002): 354–87.

Freier, Monika. 'Cultivating Emotions: The Gita Press and Its Agenda of Social and Spiritual Reform.' *South Asian History and Culture* 3, no. 3 (2012): 397–413.

Guibernau, Montserrat. *Belonging: Solidarity and Division in Modern Societies*. Cambridge: Polity, 2013.

Hogan, Patrick Colm. *What Literature Teaches Us About Emotion*. Cambridge: Cambridge University Press, 2011.

Holloway, Sally. *The Game of Love in Georgian England: Courtship, Emotions, and Material Culture*. Oxford: Oxford University Press, 2019.

Ibbett, Katherine. *Compassion's Edge: Fellow-Feeling and Its Limits in Early Modern France*. Philadelphia: University of Pennsylvania Press, 2017.

Irish, Bradley. *Emotion in the Tudor Court: Literature, History, and Early Modern Feeling*. Evanston: Northwestern University Press, 2018.

Jager, Eric. *The Book of the Heart*. Chicago: Chicago University Press, 2000.

Jalland, Pat. *Death in War and Peace: A History of Loss and Grief in England, 1914–1970*. Oxford: Oxford University Press, 2010.

Jorgensen, Alice. *Reading the Heart in the Old English Language, Literature and Culture*. Farnham: Ashgate, 2015.

Kazantzidis, George, and Dimos Spatharas, eds. *Hope in Ancient Literature, History, and Art*. Boston: De Gruyter, 2018.

Kim, Jisoo M. *The Emotions of Justice: Gender, Status and Legal Performance in Chosŏn Korea*. Seattle: University of Washington Press, 2015.

Konstan, David. *In the Orbit of Love: Affection in Ancient Greece and Rome*. Oxford: Oxford University Press, 2018.

Kotchemidova, Christina. 'From Good Cheer to "Drive-By Smiling": A Social History of Cheerfulness.' *Journal of Social History* 39, no. 1 (2005): 5–37.

Kounine, Laura. 'Emotions, Mind and Body on Trial: A Cross-Cultural Perspective.' *Journal of Social History* 51, no. 3 (2017): 219–30.

Kuijpers, Erika, and Cornelis van der Haven, eds. *Battlefield Emotions 1500– 1800: Practices, Experience, Imagination*. Basingstoke: Palgrave Macmillan, 2016.

Laffan, Michael, and Max Weiss, eds. *Facing Fear: The History of an Emotion in Global Perspective*. Princeton: Princeton University Press, 2012.

Lam, Ling Hon. *The Spatiality of Emotion in Early Modern China: From Dreamscapes to Theatricality*. New York: Columbia University Press, 2018.

Langhamer, Claire. 'Love, Selfhood and Authenticity in Post-War Britain.' *Cultural and Social History* 9, no. 2 (2012): 277–97.

Langhamer, Claire. *The English in Love: the Intimate Story of an Emotional Revolution*. Oxford: Oxford University Press, 2013.

Laube, Matthew. 'Materializing Music in the Lutheran Home.' *Past and Present* 234, no. 12 (2017): 114–38.

Lemmings, David, and Ann Brooks, eds. *Emotions and Social Change: Historical and Sociological Perspectives*. London: Routledge, 2014.

Lemmings, David, and Allyson May, eds. *"Criminal" Justice During the Long Eighteenth Century: Theatre, Representation and Emotion in the Courtroom and the Public Sphere*. London: Routledge, 2018.

Lüdtke, Alf. 'Love of State – Affection for Authority: Politics of Mass Participation in Twentieth Century European Contexts.' In *New Dangerous Liaisons: Discourses on Europe and Love in the Twentieth Century*, eds. Luisa Passerini, Liliana Ellena and Alexander C. T. Geppert, 58–74. New York: Berghahn Books, 2010.

Lyndon, Jane. 'Pity, Love or Justice? Seeing 1830s Australian Colonial Violence.' *Emotions: History, Culture, Society* 1, no. 2 (2017): 109–10.

Maddern, Philippa C., Joanne McEwan and Anne Scott, eds. *Performing Emotions in Early Modern Europe*. Turnhout: Brepols, 2018.

Marchant, Alicia, ed. *Historicising Heritage and Emotions: The Affective Histories of Blood, Stone and Land*. London: Routledge, 2019.

Maroney, Terry. 'Law and Emotion: A Proposed Taxonomy of an Emerging Field.' *Law and Human Behaviour* 30 (2006): 119–42.

Martín-Moruno, Dolores, and Beatriz Pichel, eds. *Emotional Bodies: The Historical Performativity of Emotions*. Champaign: University of Illinois Press, 2019.

Matt, Susan J. *Keeping Up with the Joneses: Envy in American Consumer Society, 1890–1930*. Philadelphia: University of Pennsylvania Press, 2003.

Matt, Susan J. *Homesickness: An American History*. Oxford: Oxford University Press, 2011.

McMahon, Darrin M. *Happiness: A History*. New York: Atlantic Monthly Press, 2006.

McNamer, Sarah. *Affective Meditation and the Invention of Medieval Compassion*. Pennsylvania: University of Pennsylvania Press, 2011.

Medick, Hans, and David Sabean, eds. *Interest and Emotion: Essays on the Study of Family and Kinship*. Cambridge: Cambridge University Press, 1984.

Meek, Richard, and Erin Sullivan, eds. *The Renaissance of Emotion: Understanding Affect in Shakespeare and His Contemporaries*. Manchester: Manchester University Press, 2015.

Menin, Marco. 'Who Will Write the History of Tears? History of Ideas and History of Emotions from the Eighteenth-Century France to the Present.' *History of European Ideas* 40, no. 4 (2014): 516–32.

Mussell, Simon. *Critical Theory and Feeling*. Manchester: Manchester University Press, 2017.

Naphy, William G., and Penny Roberts, eds. *Fear in Early Modern Society*. Manchester: Manchester University Press, 1997.

Newton, Hannah. *Misery & Mirth: Recovery from Illness in Early Modern England*. Oxford: Oxford University Press, 2018.

Pantti, Mervi, Karin Wahl-Jorgensen and Simon Cottles, eds. *Disasters and the Media*. New York: Peter Lang, 2012.

Payne, Linda. *With Words and Knives: Learning Medical Dispassion in Early Modern England*. London: Routledge, 2016.

Pearsall, Sarah M. S. '"The Power of Feeling"? Emotion, Sensibility, and the American Revolution.' *Modern Intellectual History* 8, no. 3 (2011): 659–72.

Perler, Dominick, *Feelings Transformed: Philosophical Theories of the Emotions, 1270–1670*, trans. Tony Crawford. Oxford: Oxford University Press, 2018.

Pinto, Sarah. 'The History of Emotions in Australia.' *Australian Historical Studies* 48, no. 1 (2017): 103–14.

Pollock, Linda. 'Anger and the Negotiation of Relationships in Early Modern England.' *Historical Journal* 47 (2004): 567–90.

Potkay, Adam. *The Story of Joy: From the Bible to Late Romanticism*. Cambridge: Cambridge University Press, 2007.

Prendergast, Thomas, and Stephanie J. Trigg. *Affective Medievalism: Love, Abjection and Discontent*. Manchester: Manchester University Press, 2018.

Price, Brian. *A Theory of Regret*. Durham: Duke University Press, 2017.

Reckwitz, Andreas. 'Affective Spaces: A Praxeological Outlook.' *Rethinking History* 16, no. 2 (2012): 241–58.

Reddy, William M. *The Making of Romantic Love: Longing and Sexuality in Europe, South Asia, and Japan, 900–1200 CE*. Chicago: University of Chicago Press, 2012.

Reid, Richard. 'Mourning and Glory: Toward Affective Histories of Violence in Africa over *la Longue Durée*.' *Emotions: History, Culture, Society* 1, no. 1 (2017): 113–36.

Robin, Corey. *Fear: The History of a Political Idea*. Oxford: Oxford University Press, 2004.

Robinson, Emily. 'Touching the Void: Affective History and the Impossible.' *Rethinking History* 14, no. 4 (2010): 503–20.

Rodman, Margaret Critchlow. 'The Heart in the Archives: Colonial Contestation of Desire and Fear in the New Hebrides, 1933.' *Journal of Pacific History* 38, no. 3 (2003): 291–312.

Rosenfeld, Sophia. 'Thinking About Feeling, 1789–1799.' *French Historical Studies* 32, no. 4 (2009): 697–706.

Rosenwein, Barbara H., ed. *Anger's Past: The Social Uses of an Emotion in the Middle Ages*. Ithaca, NY: Cornell University Press, 1998.

Rüsen, Jörn. 'Emotional Forces in Historical Thinking: Some Metahistorical Reflections and the Case of Mourning.' *Historein: A Review of the Past and Other Stories* 8 (2008): 41–53.

Santangelo, Paolo, and Donatella Guida, eds. *Love, Hatred, and Other Passions: Questions and Themes on Emotions in Chinese Civilization*. Leiden: Brill, 2006.

Santangelo, Paolo, and Ulrike Middendorf, eds. *From Skin to Heart: Perceptions of Emotions and Bodily Sensations in Traditional Chinese Culture*. Wiesbaden: Harrassowitz, 2006.

Scheff, Thomas J. *Bloody Revenge: Emotions, Nationalism, and War*. Boulder: Westview Press, 1994.

Scott, Anne, and Cynthia Kosso, eds. *Fear and Its Representations in the Middle Ages and Renaissance*. Turnhout: Brepols, 2002.

Sedgwick, Eve Kosofsky. *Touching Feeling: Affect, Pedagogy, Performativity*. Durham: Duke University Press, 2003.

Smith, Mick, Joyce Davidson, Laura Cameron and Liz Bondi, eds. *Emotion, Place, Culture*. London: Routledge, 2016.

Sontag, Susan. *Regarding the Pain of Others*. New York: Picador, 2004.

Stauffer, Andrew M. *Anger, Revolution and Romanticism*. Cambridge, Cambridge University Press, 2005.

Stearns, Peter N. *Shame: A Brief History*. Champaign: University of Illinois Press, 2017.

Steenbergh, Kristine. 'Green Wounds: Pain, Anger and Revenge in Early Modern Culture.' In *The Sense of Suffering: Constructions of Physical Pain in Early Modern Culture*, eds. J. F. van Dijkhuizen, and K. A. E. Enenkel, 165–88. Leiden: Brill, 2009.

Steenbergh, Kristine. 'Compassion and the Creation of an Affective Community in the Theatre: Vondel's Mary Stuart or Martyred Majesty (1646).' *Low Countries Historical Review* 129, no. 2 (2014): 90–112.

Steinberg, Mark D., and Valeria Sobol. *Interpreting Emotions in Russia and Eastern Europe*. Illinois: Northern Illinois University Press, 2011.

Strange, Carolyn, Robert Cribb and Christopher E. Forth, eds. *Honour, Violence and Emotions in History*. London: Bloomsbury, 2014.

Sullivan, Erin. 'The History of the Emotions: Past, Present, Future.' *Cultural History* 2, no. 1 (2013): 93–102.

Thorley, David. 'Towards a History of Emotions, 1562–1660.' *The Seventeenth Century* 28, no. 1 (2013): 3–19.

Twells, Alison. '"Went into Raptures": Reading Emotion in the Ordinary Wartime Diary, 1941–1946.' *Women's History Review* 25, no. 1 (2016): 143–60.

Tyson, Amy M. *The Wages of History: Emotional Labor on Public History's Front Lines*. Amherst: University of Massachusetts Press, 2013.

Vincent-Buffault, Anne. *The History of Tears: Sensibility and Sentimentality in France*. New York: St. Martin's Press, 1991.

Virág, Curie. 'Emotions and Human Agency in the Thought of Zhu Xi.' *Journal of Song Yuan Studies* 37 (2007): 49–88.

White, R. S., Katrina O'Loughlin and Mark Houlahan, eds. *Shakespeare and Emotions: Inheritances, Enactments, Legacies*. Basingstoke: Palgrave Macmillan, 2015.

Wickberg, Daniel. 'What Is the History of Sensibilities? On Cultural Histories, Old and New.' *American Historical Review* 112, no. 3 (2007): 661–84.

Zeldin, Theodore. 'Personal History and the History of Emotions.' *Journal of Social History* 15, no. 3 (1982): 339–47.

Notes

CHAPTER 1

1. Thomas Dixon, *From Passions to Emotions: the Creation of a Secular Psychological Category* (Cambridge: Cambridge University Press, 2003).
2. Giovanna Coolombetti, *The Feeling Body: Affective Science Meets the Enactive Mind* (Cambridge: The MIT Press, 2014).
3. Katie Barclay, 'New Materialism and The New History of the Emotions,' *Emotions: History, Culture, Society* 1, no. 1 (2017): 161–83.
4. Monique Scheer, 'Are Emotions a Kind of Practice (and Is That What Makes Them Have a History)? A Bourdieuian Approach to Understanding Emotion,' *History & Theory* 51, no. 2 (2012): 190–220.
5. William Reddy, *The Navigation of Feeling: A Framework for the History of Emotions* (Cambridge: Cambridge University Press, 2001).
6. Steven Connor, 'Collective Emotions: Reasons to Feel Doubtful,' The History of Emotions annual lecture given at Queen Mary, University of London, 9 October 2013; Christian von Scheve, 'Collective Emotions in Rituals: Elicitations, Transmission, and a "Mathew-effect,"' in *Emotions in Rituals*, ed. A. Michaels and C. Wulf (London: Routledge, 2011), 55–77.
7. Sara Ahmed, *The Cultural Politics of Emotion* (Edinburgh: Edinburgh University Press, 2004).
8. Kirk Essary, 'Passions, Affections, or Emotions? On the Ambiguity of 16th-Century Terminology,' *Emotion Review* 9, no. 4 (2017): 367–74.
9. Thomas Dixon, 'Angers Past, or Anger's Past,' Histories of Emotion, https://historiesofemotion.com/2016/12/09/angers-past-or-angers-past/?platform=hootsuite, accessed 15 September 2019.

CHAPTER 2

1. For a survey see: Katie Barclay, 'The Emotional Lives of Wedding Certificates,' *Cultural and Social History* (online first 2019), https://doi.org/10.1080/14780038.2019.1589156.
2. *The Complete Letter-Writer, containing Familiar Letters on the Most Common Occasions in Life* (Edinburgh, 1789), 59.

3. Ibid., 136–37.
4. National Records of Scotland, Edinburgh, Papers of Gilbert Innes of Stowe, GD113/5/491/16.
5. Dr Williams Library, London, Doddridge Collection, L1/1.
6. *The Writings and Speeches of Daniel Webster: Private Correspondence edited by Fletcher Webster*, 18 volumes (Boston: Little, Brown & Co, 1903), vol. 1, 71.
7. Ibid., 80–82.
8. Ibid., 132.
9. Ibid., 153–4.

CHAPTER 3

1. Peter N. Stearns with Carol Z. Stearns, 'Emotionology: Clarifying the History of Emotions and Emotional Standards,' *The American Historical Review* 90, no. 4 (1985): 813–36.
2. Peter Stearns, *American Cool: Constructing a Twentieth-Century Emotional Style* (New York: New York University Press, 1994).
3. Arlie Russell Hochschild, *The Managed Heart: Commercialization of Human Feeling (Berkeley: University of California Press. 1983)*.
4. Thomas Dixon, *Weeping Britannia: Portrait of a Nation in Tears* (Oxford: Oxford University Press, 2015).

CHAPTER 4

1. Barbara Rosenwein, 'Worrying about Emotions in History,' *American Historical Review* 107, no. 3 (2002): 842.
2. Mark Seymour, 'Emotional Arenas: From Provincial Circus to National Courtroom in Late Nineteenth-Century Italy,' *Rethinking History* 16, no. 2 (2012): 177–97.
3. Having said this, I think the theory itself is flexible enough to allow this to happen if such a community existed.

CHAPTER 5

1. Erin Sullivan, *Beyond Melancholy: Sadness and Selfhood in Renaissance England* (Oxford: Oxford University Press, 2016), 9.

2. William M. Reddy, *The Navigation of Feeling: A Framework for the History of Emotions* (Cambridge: Cambridge University Press, 2001), 129.
3. Rob Boddice, *The History of Emotions* (Manchester: Manchester University Press, 2018), 69–70.

CHAPTER 6

1. Alexandra Walsham, 'Recycling the Sacred: Material Culture and Cultural Reformation after the English Reformation,' *Church History* 86, no. 4 (2017): 1121–54.
2. For more information see: www.metmuseum.org/art/collection/search/464300.
3. For more information see: https://wellcomecollection.org/works/ytv2bjka.
4. For more information see: https://wellcomecollection.org/works/hh2w5g6j.
5. For more information see: www.metmuseum.org/art/collection/search/193661.
6. For more information see: www.metmuseum.org/art/collection/search/193674.
7. For more information see: https://inpress.lib.uiowa.edu/feminae/DetailsPage.aspx?Feminae_ID=39007; www.metmuseum.org/art/collection/search/464128.
8. For more information see: www.metmuseum.org/art/collection/search/464334.

CHAPTER 7

1. The full report can be read here: https://archive.org/details/ape9901.0001.001.umich.edu/page/n9
2. Civil lines refer to the residential neighbourhoods created for White colonial officers and their families in Indian towns.

Index

9 781352 010350